# NIGHT GAMES

## A JOURNEY TO THE DARK SIDE OF SPORT

# ANNA KRIEN

YELLOW JERSEY PRESS

LONDON

Vintage is part of the Penguin Random House group of companies
whose addresses can be found at global.penguinrandomhouse.com

 Penguin
Random House
UK

First published in Great Britain in 2014 by
Yellow Jersey Press

First published in Australia in 2013 by
Black Inc., an imprint of Schwartz Media Pty Ltd

www.vintage-books.co.uk

A CIP catalogue record for this book is
available from the British Library

ISBN 9780224100038

Printed and bound by CPI Group (UK) Ltd, Croydon, CR0 4YY

 MIX
Paper from
responsible sources
FSC
www.fsc.org  FSC® C018179

Penguin Random House is committed to a sustainable future
for our business, our readers and our planet. This book is made
from Forest Stewardship Council® certified paper.

# CONTENTS

# AUTHOR'S NOTE

I have changed the name of the defendant in the following account of a rape trial. On grounds of confidentiality I am not permitted to give the complainant's name, and in fairness I believe the defendant's name should be suppressed here for the same reason. Several other names have also been changed.

As is customary in rape trials, the complainant's evidence was given in closed court and cannot be reported.

# PROLOGUE

When the members of the jury – ten men and two women – emerge from the back room, they don't look at him. Their eyes do a darting sweep of the court, lifting up and over our outlines. The defendant's seats are full, the complainant's seats behind the prosecutor – except for a lone policewoman who has arrived to hear the verdict – are empty, as they have been since the beginning of the trial, and the press seats – where I am – are largely vacant.

Five days ago there had been barely any standing room as the reporters crammed in, opening and shutting the door in the middle of proceedings. A star footballer had arrived to give evidence. The Collingwood player took the stand jauntily, swinging a little in his chair as he spoke.

Today it's just an ordinary man in the dock, his face grey with dread, eyes rimmed red, no big deal as far as headlines are concerned. 'He's not a footballer at all,' the judge and prosecution had agreed before the jury was selected and the trial commenced. I turned to look at Justin Dyer then. Disbelief flickered across his face. He'd been dropped from his team in the Victorian Football League after the charges were laid.

'No, he's a hanger-on,' said the prosecution.

'Exactly,' said the judge.

'Have you reached your verdict?' the judge now enquires. The foreman of the jury nods and stands up. The 23-year-old in the dock is answering to six counts: one of indecent assault, the rest – rape.

'Not guilty.'

Justin buckles and lets out a huge wracking sob. His gasps seem to heave over his cordoned-off area, over the wooden banister, to his family. They let out a choking sound. The jury foreman trails off, looking at the man in the dock, the document in his hand shaking.

The judge nods at him to continue, and with each verdict of not guilty the sobbing grows louder, the family now holding themselves, arms crossed over one another, as if forming a kind of dinghy on a rough sea and taking the waves of Justin's gasping as their own.

The jury members shift in their seats, fiddling with their hands, with the rings on their fingers, stealing wide-eyed looks at the dock. It is as if they are seeing Justin for the first time.

With my fingers, I try to push my own tears back into the seams of my eyes. I squeeze my nails into my palms, etching the skin, for distraction. The solicitor for the state, bringing to the court the charges initiated by Sarah Wesley, the complainant, sits facing the court. She exchanges a long, knowing look with the policewoman in the front row behind the Crown prosecutor.

As the jury is thanked and dismissed, I stare at my notepad. 'Now they know the difference between what is said in popular media and reality,' the judge says of the jurors to the lawyers. We all try to ignore the whirlpool of emotion in the corner of the room.

After the judge departs, the reporters stand awkwardly at the door, waiting for the family to settle, to sort themselves out and start leaving so they can ask for a quote or two. I stand with them, but I don't really belong. I know this family now. I've sat with them outside for the past three weeks, waiting with them in that dead space. I put my pencil and notebook away, take a deep breath and cross over the empty seats into this flooding family on the defendant's side.

His grandmother envelops me in a hug and I think, well, there goes my objectivity. And I'm struggling with this. It's as if I'm inside out. The journalists at the door, their faces are unreadable, they have cool exteriors. I admire their poise, their unmuddied positions, absolved in their detachment. It's all backwards for me. Because despite the verdict, I still don't know who is guilty and who is innocent, and yet here I am, hugging the grandmother in the defendant's corner, and that's a problem, don't you think?

# PART I
# THE FOOTY SHOW

# CHAPTER I

Much like the federal election of 2010, the Australian Rules Football grand final that year was a draw. It was an unfathomable concept for players and spectators: how do you party when there are no winners and no losers? Then, to the delight of pubs, merchandise sellers and sausage makers, the Australian Football League announced a rematch between Collingwood and St Kilda. The Pies beat the Saints and the city of Melbourne was still cloaked in black and white crepe paper when the rumour of a pack rape by celebrating footballers began to surface. By morning, the head of the Victorian sexual crimes squad confirmed to journalists that they were preparing to question two Collingwood players, the young recruits Dayne Beams and John McCarthy. And so, as police were confiscating bedsheets from a townhouse in Dorcas Street, South Melbourne, the trial by media began.

'Yet another alleged girl, making alleged allegations, after she awoke with an alleged hangover and I take it an alleged guilty conscience,' the retired footballer Peter 'Spida' Everitt announced on Twitter, and followed it up with 'Girls!! When will you learn! At 3am when you are blind drunk & you decide to go home with a guy ITS NOT FOR A CUP OF MILO!' The morning TV host Kerri-Anne Kennerley picked up the thread, sympathising with players, saying that they 'put themselves in harm's way by picking up strays.'

When Justin Dyer first had an inkling that the weekend he'd had was going to be turned upside down – and it had been a good one too, grand final day, his mates had won, he'd picked up that night, gone one up in the 'rooting competition' he was having with his mates – he was driving to work in his ute, carpentry tools in the tray. Beams's housemate called him on his mobile and said, that girl, she's gone to the cops, said she's been raped.

The rest of the drive was surreal, said Justin.

Then he got another call, this time from Beams, who said the cops were going to call him and not to say anything. To call Dale Curtis, Collingwood's director of legal counsel, instead. From there, Justin was put in touch with David Galbally QC, the club's lawyer. 'I went to Galbally and wrote up my statement to take to the police. He said you're a witness, not a suspect.' But when he arrived at the station, police told him he was a suspect. 'I felt sick. I kept wondering if this was really happening. Her original complaint was about Collingwood and then I came along.'

When Justin was charged with six counts of rape, one of attempted rape and one of indecent assault, Galbally told the Melbourne Magistrates' Court that his client would contest the charges. At this, a few astute observers on AFL forums pricked up their ears. 'Why is Dave Galbally QC the defendant's lawyer?' asked one commentator.

Apart from being friends with Dayne Beams – they had played together back in Queensland – Justin had nothing to do with Collingwood Football Club. The club he was playing for in the state league, the Coburg Tigers, was affiliated with Richmond, and rather than offer support Coburg decided to drop him. The board called him to a meeting and said, 'You're never going to get another game here.'

Justin was a small fish in big trouble. He knew no one. He was twenty-two years old, had recently broken up with his girlfriend of four years and was living out of home for the first time. He and a mate had driven to Melbourne ten months earlier, to the home of Aussie Rules, where the two midfielders could play footy closer to the roving eyes of talent scouts. So, when the shit hit, he was grateful to find himself tucked under the arm of Galbally, despite not really knowing why.

But with Beams and McCarthy not yet in the clear, the reason for the QC's presence seemed pretty obvious to an outsider like me. It made sense to control the narrative. Dyer was a nobody, but what had happened that night and how it revealed itself could affect 'real' footballers, not to mention the richest footy club in town.

Other things about the case interested me, too. There was the girl, Sarah Wesley.

*

Over a decade ago, in the front bar of a pub in North Fitzroy, I listened to the pub trivia going on in the back room. 'What was the name of the girl who died in a hotel room with Gary Ablett?'

I remember sucking in the air as though I'd been punched. Surely this isn't pub trivia, I thought, then just as quickly I prayed that someone would remember her name, the twenty-year-old footy fan who lay comatose from a drug overdose in Melbourne's Hyatt hotel while forty-year-old Ablett Senior, known as 'God' to his admirers, called an ambulance and then did a runner, hiding out with his manager, Ricky Nixon. For hours the girl was simply a 'Jane Doe' in the hospital.

'Horan!' one guy yelled. 'Alisha Horan!' His trivia team whooped.

I wrote the incident down on the back of a beer coaster.

Three years later, in 2003, two sports journalists at the *Sydney Morning Herald*, Jacquelin Magnay and Jessica Halloran, wrote about the 'Dark Side of the Game,' revealing a culture of sharing women in rugby league. Describing 'gangbangs' as a rite of passage, the reporters highlighted two incidents.

A 42-year-old Coffs Harbour woman had laid a sexual assault complaint against the Canterbury Bulldogs. She said she had consented to sex with one player when they visited her home-town, but not a second, while a third had been in the room as an 'observer.'

The second incident, which later became infamous on the ABC's *Four Corners*, involved the Cronulla Sharks' trip to New Zealand and a nineteen-year-old female hotel employee. Magnay and Halloran wrote: 'After the Sharks complaint, one club called a team meeting and warned its players not to share women. After the Bulldogs incident, an official at another club told its players "to make sure the woman leaves happy and then she won't complain."'

Following the article's appearance, the National Rugby League's then chief executive, David Gallop, wrote a five-page letter of outraged complaint to the *Sydney Morning Herald*'s publisher. Magnay, who has covered rugby league on and off for almost two decades, said the scepticism about the story, and the impulse to dismiss it or 'shoot the messenger,' was maddening. 'At the time, we were perceived as troublemakers, as if we were making it up, that we were fantasists. It really annoyed me that we were not being taken seriously and people considered what we wrote to be so trivial.'

Then, twelve months later, the Canterbury Bulldogs were involved in another incident at Coffs Harbour. A brawl broke out at the Plantation Hotel after locals took exception to players groping women on the dance floor. By morning a 21-year-old woman had been taken to hospital in an ambulance, claiming that up to eight players had raped her. They were staying at the same hotel where the 42-year-old woman had made her allegation – her case having been subsequently dropped by the director of public prosecutions because, like so many rape complaints, it boiled down to the woman's word against that of the players.

Agreeing to speak to *60 Minutes*, the 42-year-old woman, 'Kate,' who still lived in the town, described her reaction on hearing the new allegations on the radio:

It just sort of threw me back, bang, and I started, nervous, I was like sort of really shaking, thinking that they've actually done it again. And how dare they even think to come back to Coffs Harbour where they were staying and just do it again, just exactly the same.

She went on to describe the night that had led her to the police. She had agreed to have sex with a player at the Pacific Bay Resort. 'I consented to that and I had no problems there,' she said. 'He went downstairs … I thought he was going to get a glass of water.' When he returned, the lights were out and the room was dark. 'I didn't sort of have face-to-face contact with him … as we were having sex on the bed [a second time] I saw a flash or a shadow from the side of me and as I've looked up there was another footballer … standing there masturbating. So I've quickly turned around and moved what I thought was [name deleted] away from me and it wasn't [him].'

Kate said she started screaming and yelling, gathered up her things and fled the apartment. She was followed by the player she'd originally consented to have sex with, who now pleaded with her not to go to the police, that it would ruin his reputation, that he had a new wife and baby. As she sat in the gutter, crying, two club officials approached her.

> They said, 'Well, what's happening, what's going on?' And I gave them the rundown and one of the officials, he said to me straight out, 'Well, is this a habit of yours? Do you always go out doing this sort of thing?' … I said, 'I'm going to go to the police.' And they said, 'Oh, no, no, no, don't go to the police, we'll deal with it, we'll deal with it in our tribunal, they won't get away with it, you know, please just write us your statement and we'll deal with it.'

When news of the second Coffs Harbour incident surfaced, Magnay rang David Gallop for a comment. The first thing he said to her was, 'Are you going to say I told you so?'

'He'd obviously been mulling over it for some time and come to the conclusion, whether these new allegations were true or false, that there was a serious problem,' Magnay told me.

The Bulldogs, on the other hand, quickly closed ranks. The club's football manager selected four players to speak to the police that Sunday and then they all flew home to Sydney. On Tuesday, after training, the players and club management met in private to discuss what had gone on at Coffs. This discussion became known as the 'truth meeting' or, as critics put it, the 'let's get our stories straight' meeting. The players reacted angrily to the media scrutiny, complaining they were being portrayed as a 'bunch of rapists.' At a training session as the team ran past journalists and photographers, one player yelled that they should 'pull their dicks out and come all over them.' In Coffs Harbour, a sign saying 'Charge the Dirty Dogs' was hung on an overpass over a local road.

Down south, the AFL was no doubt holding its breath, praying for the ensuing storm to pass them by. It didn't.

Less than a month later, in March 2004, police questioned two St Kilda players, Stephen Milne and Leigh Montagna, over the alleged rape of a nineteen-year-old girl. The girl claimed to have been on the receiving end of a now disturbingly familiar 'prank,' telling police that at one stage in the night she thought it was Montagna trying to have sex with her again. She repeatedly said, 'No.' When the man kept trying against her wishes, she realised the two men had 'swapped' partners in the dark. She ran from the room. Milne later pleaded guilty to indecent assault after the rape charges were dropped.

It was now official: something dark and malicious had seeded itself within football culture. Sensing a shift in public perception, the chiefs of the Australian Football League and the National Rugby League decided to acknowledge the problem. The AFL's chief executive, Andrew Demetriou, called on women to come forward with their stories, while David Gallop put together a team to produce a plan to change the attitude of league footballers towards women. The team included a feminist academic, Dr Catharine Lumby, the manager of the NSW Rape Crisis Centre, Karen Willis, and a writer and queer politics educator, Dr Kath Albury. 'He could have hired a public relations firm,' Lumby told me, 'but he hired us instead.'

*

The game has changed. Whomever you talk to in the world of Aussie Rules says as much. For some people – such as indigenous players – that's a good thing. Following the introduction of its policy against racial and religious vilification in 1995, the AFL can now boast that more than 10 per cent of its players are indigenous, substantially more than the 2 per cent of the larger population that is indigenous. But for others, well, football just ain't like it used to be.

In a *Herald Sun* Q&A column in 2011, the sports journalist Jon Anderson and a former Carlton player, David Rhys-Jones, bemoaned the passing of the glory days. 'In many ways I feel sorry for today's players,' said Rhys-Jones. 'Okay, they get the money, but do they have the fun? No way.' Back then, he said, journalists rolled around in the 'same drip tray' as the footballers. Anderson chipped in with a memory. Remember when someone let loose with the fire extinguisher at Brian 'The Whale' Roberts' pub? Sigh.

If the moment can be pinpointed when some footballers' respect, or lack of it, for their fellow human beings first came under serious scrutiny, it was in 1993, when Nicky Winmar responded to on-field racist abuse by lifting his jersey and pointing to his black skin. The photograph of that event is now iconic. This defiant act, said the footballer Andrew McLeod at a recent United Nations forum on racism in sport, 'made the AFL sit up and take notice.' Two years later, the racial vilification policy was rolled out across the league and extended to every football competition in Australia.

While the new rules soon became a source of pride for some, to others they signified the disinheritance of a certain type of footy culture. Criticising Demetriou's 2004 call for women to come forward, John Elliott, the former president of the Carlton Football Club for twenty years, said the AFL was opening up a 'Pandora's Box.' Elliott claimed that while he was president of Carlton during the eighties and nineties, the club had paid at least four women $5000 each to dissuade them from making public claims of sexual assault.

I think we had people who claimed to be raped by our players – women they were, not men – on four or five occasions. Not once did any of those stories get into the press because in those days we probably had only twenty people writing in the press and they weren't interested in all that sort of nonsense. We'd pay the sheilas off and wouldn't hear another word.

Elliott, also a former leading businessman and Liberal Party president, implied that many women had been paid by clubs to keep their silence in settlements now referred to as 'hush money.' The past had been paid for, he believed, no point in revisiting it.

And so, as the codes strove to do the right thing, it became clear that something or someone was resisting.

Back in 1995, when the football personality Sam Newman impersonated Nicky Winmar by 'blacking up' on *The Footy Show,* it was a way of saying 'up yours' to the new racial and religious vilification policy. A decade later, as the AFL rolled out its Respect & Responsibility program towards women, *The Footy Show* responded with another 'harmless' prank.

On live television, Newman staple-gunned a photo of the *Age*'s senior football journalist Caroline Wilson to a mannequin's head. The mannequin was wearing a satin bra and underpants. 'I tell you what, she's a fair piece, Caro,' he said, standing back to admire the dummy. As he held up items of clothing, fumbling around the breasts, one of the show's hosts, Garry Lyon, laughed and wrung his hands.

'You getting nervous about this?' asked Newman, as he approached Wilson's teeth with a black texta. 'Garry – can I just say something, Garry?' he continued. 'We're only having fun … and I know you're getting nervous about it, but we're only having fun. If you're on our show, you're on our show –'

'We are!' yelped Lyon, shifting uncomfortably in his seat. The studio audience whooped and cheered for Newman. 'We are!' Lyon said again.

Consciously or unconsciously, Newman's gag and many others like it were designed to pull down these new values.

Newman tested Lyon's loyalty on air, later defending the mannequin gag as a kind of 'male' compliment. It was a sign, he said, that
*The Footy Show*, aka Sam Newman, accepted Caroline Wilson.
And this gets us to the crux of the problem, not just with Aussie
Rules and Rugby League, but also with American football,
European soccer – turn the ball into a puck, put a stick in their
hands, and it's a problem in ice hockey. The problem is not the
game per se, but the macho culture of humiliation that tends to
shadow and control it.

# CHAPTER 2

David Galbally surveyed the Magistrates' Court with the assurance of a top predator. His hawkish features, sharp blue eyes and ruffle of silver hair put the court to a kind of clunky shame. The prosecutor appeared on the back foot, he hadn't got copies of this or that, his hair was a mess and his suit untidy. While he was blustering through his papers, Galbally was at ease, making jokes, working the room. I was at Justin Dyer's committal hearing, a mini-trial compressed into two days in July 2011, a brief parade of witnesses for the magistrate to test if there was sufficient evidence to take the charges to trial.

In a light grey suit, Justin sat silently behind his lawyer, his parents beside him. He watched as people appeared on the stand – apparitions from a solitary Saturday night nine months ago. People he knew, others he'd seen that night also partying but didn't know – friends of friends, friends of hers, there was even the taxi driver who had driven him home – all lined up to weave their fading fragments of a night into a single narrative.

And finally, she was there, not physically but on a screen.

Later I asked Justin how he felt seeing her, if he had changed the way she looked in his mind. After all, he'd only met her that once. A quiet man, Justin shrugged. 'I don't know, I was angry.'

It was seven and a half months since Justin Dyer had been charged with the rape of Sarah Wesley. He had first been summoned to court six weeks after the grand final celebrations. Camera crews and reporters had crowded around him, the footage later rolling on the evening news while newspapers immediately posted photos of him online.

In one photo, he looked defiant, head held high, eyes slit thin like the gaps in a venetian blind – but those slivers revealed nothing, they were glassy, shadowed and unfathomable. Pale skin, the kind of stubble that re-emerges five seconds after a shave, his brown hair trimmed in a typical barber's cut – short sides, long top.

What was most striking about the image was Justin's lone figure. He was without his team, carefully cut out from the pack – the story being as much about who wasn't in the photo as who was. And while none of the news media said as much, the innuendo was there – the initial police leak had suggested an evening with several protagonists, so where were the others?

On a post-season training camp in Arizona apparently.

Six weeks had passed since Sarah's initial police report. Beams and McCarthy were not yet in the clear, but as Justin fronted up to court to hear his charges, they were completing high-altitude training with Collingwood. The police were still investigating the young players, but so far rounding up Justin had been easier.

Once the charges were laid, photos of Justin had multiplied on the internet – walking with his mother from court, emerging with his lawyers through a glass revolving door – and each time he appeared steely, a shell. But a scrum of cameras can do that.

\*

Galbally handed a young redheaded man in the witness box a copy of his original police statement and asked him to read out the highlighted portion to the magistrate, which he did:

> I asked her if she had sex with Nate because I knew she went home with him. She said she did and then I asked what happened. It took a while for her to get it all out. I knew something was wrong because I'd never seen her crying like this ... Then she said there were Collingwood footballers there. She repeated she had sex with Nate and that while she was having sex with Nate he couldn't get an erection. Then she said she had Beams on one side and Nate on the other ...

This was Tom Shaw reading. Studying law, he lived at the same residential college as Sarah. His room was one down from hers and they were good friends. Best friends, even. Sarah had celebrated her twenty-first birthday not long before the events and Tom had made one of the speeches.

Shaw told the court how he, Sarah and another friend, Olivia, got ready to go out that Saturday evening. Pouring Red Bull and vodkas, they went back and forth between each other's rooms, playing different tunes on a laptop. Sarah was wanting to meet up with Nate Cooper, a VFL player she had met two weeks before at the Turf Bar, and so the three of them were planning to head to Prahran where he was at a party. But then she got word he was on his way to Eve nightclub in South Melbourne, so they went there instead. Olivia, who wasn't drinking, was driving.

It was about midnight as they queued to get into Eve, and Tom reckoned they – he and Sarah – sobered up a little in the cool air. Tall, blonde and striking, Sarah was in a colourful dress and strappy high-heel sandals, her legs bare and a small black purse slung across her shoulder. Tom was wearing – well, who cares? Inside, it was rounds of raspberry vodkas, dancing, and the three lost sight of each other. Around 5 a.m., Tom was trying to get in touch with Sarah on his phone and then Olivia received a text from her saying she had gone home with Nate.

The next morning Sarah called Tom, crying, and he went to her room.

'She detailed and complained about the fact that she had sex with these people, Nate and these other people, in the room?' asked Galbally. 'She was telling you that she had sex against her will?'

Tom nodded. 'Yes.'

'And that she was effectively raped by them?'

'Yes.'

Galbally continued: 'Alright, then you detail everything else that she said to you. At that point in time the names that she mentions to you are primarily, well, are Nate, Beams and Macca?'

'Yes.'

Sarah knew only the nicknames of the men and that they were from Collingwood. So Tom got his laptop out and brought up Nate's Facebook page and typed 'Beams' into the Collingwood website.

Galbally again: 'And she told you that there are a number of males coming in and out of the room?'

'Yes.'

'And did she tell you that those males were naked?'

'Not at that time.'

'Did she tell you at a later time that they were naked?'

'Someone had their pants around their ankles, yes.'

By this stage, as Tom sat with Sarah in her room, laptop open on the bed, her parents were on their way to the college. Soon Olivia, who lived nearby, would be there too. In this time, Sarah hadn't mentioned Justin to Tom. But then his name flashed up on the screen of her phone. It was a call that simultaneously drew Justin into the allegations but also made them far from clear-cut. Tom picked up Sarah's phone and answered.

Not realising that it wasn't her on the line, Justin said, 'Hi, it's Justin. From last night.'

There was a pause until Tom said, 'It's Tom, Sarah's friend.'

Justin explained that he was checking to see if Sarah had got home okay, that he had put her in a taxi. Tom thanked him. They hung up.

Soon after Sarah called the police.

\*

When the policewoman in charge of the investigation, Detective Senior Constable Christine Stafford, took the stand, Galbally read from her original notes, asking her to confirm them.

'"Had consented sex with Nate" … then goes on to say "Nate

introduces victim to Dayne Beams"?'

The policewoman, her finger tracing the words in her notebook in front of her, nodded. 'Correct.'

'"Then Collingwood player, felt compelled to have sex but … not forced." Not forced?'

'Correct.'

'"Two to four other naked males in the room?"'

'Correct.'

'"Then they grab her and force her to perform oral sex on male and vaginal rape?"'

'Correct.'

'"Remember saying 'No'?"'

'Correct.'

'"Felt trapped."'

Stafford nodded again and repeated after him, 'Felt trapped.'

Yet despite the allegations Sarah made against the young men in the South Melbourne townhouse, it emerged that the police had wound up their investigation of the two Magpie players six months before today's hearing, deciding not to lay any charges. Instead Justin was charged with raping Sarah in an alleyway after she left the townhouse. The difficulty was this: how to discuss what had happened in the alley without referring to the incident in the bedroom some 500 metres away? And had Justin been in the bedroom? Was he under the impression that Sarah was happy to 'do the rounds'?

When the reporters present at the committal hearing discovered that the two Collingwood footballers wouldn't be called to give evidence for the time being, they gathered up their things and made for the elevators.

One veteran journalist, noticing I was going to stick around, said disbelievingly, 'You don't really think there's something in this, do you?'

I shrugged, and then gestured at the Collingwood lawyer in a huddle with Justin and his parents in the foyer. 'Then why is he still here?' I said quietly, nodding towards Galbally.

The journalist looked at Galbally, who was doing all the talking while the Dyer family listened, and then back at me. 'You think it's some kind of conspiracy?'

I recoiled. 'No, of course not.'

The journalist smiled at me and said goodbye. I sat down and watched the huddle, the pale-faced Justin intently listening to Galbally as he would to a coach. *Conspiracy.* It was definitely not the word I was looking for. After all, Galbally was looking after his client – that was clear as you watched him in action. But at the same time, the lawyer had succeeded in keeping the star footballers from attending the hearing, while every other bit player from the evening had appeared.

And now the entire bedroom episode was being sidelined. I couldn't help wondering why Justin was the only one left facing charges.

'Does it matter?' a former policeman said to me when I rang him to ask how police decide *whom* to charge when there are not only several events, but also several people involved.

I was unsure. 'What if someone is potentially more guilty than another?'

'Guilty is guilty,' he replied.

Towards the end of the committal, the prosecution called Kathy Hackett to the stand. Hackett was living in a house in one of a few alleyways that came off the street that Sarah and Justin had walked along to get a cab. Responding to a police door-knock, Hackett said she'd heard something outside her bedroom window, and the police soon decided that it was her alley where the alleged rape had occurred.

'I felt sick to the stomach when I heard what happened,' Hackett said boldly on the stand.

I sat up sharply. Had she heard about 'what happened' before she spoke to police, or worse, did the police tell her what they were investigating before they took her statement?

Hackett told the court that she had been sleeping that morning when she heard people outside her window. It was 'muffled,' she said, and she thought she heard someone say, 'No, stop it.'

'Now, is there anything you want to clarify or add or change to your statement that you made?' asked the prosecution.

Hackett nodded. 'Just as when, when I thought about after I spoke to the police that I could have swore I heard, um, clip-clop noises, noises like she was running away.'

'Right, so what you said you heard – clip-clop noises. When did you hear those?'

'After whatever because I'd – I'd heard her go off.'

I didn't realise it to begin with, but my mouth was hanging open. I looked around the courtroom, trying to catch some-one's eye.

Is this for real? I wanted to say. This can't be taken seriously: surely the further away you are from an event, the less you remember – not more.

*

After a break, we returned to the courtroom to hear the magistrate's decision. Justin was asked to stand. The magistrate cleared his throat and announced that the case would be going to trial. The Dyer family looked stunned. The evidence had seemed so flimsy, mostly the recollections of drunk twenty-year-olds and then Hackett with her recent recollection of clip-clop sounds. But then there was Sarah's evidence in closed court: what had she said? Was it credible? The magistrate must have thought so. Justin was going to trial early next year and although the Dyer family didn't know it yet, David Galbally wouldn't be accompanying them.

# CHAPTER 3

'It flows into the record of interview, it flows all over the place, Your Honour,' said Malcolm Thomas, Justin's new defence counsel. 'It flows into complaint evidence, it flows into medical evidence.'

It was day one of Justin's trial. He sat silently in the dock, watching as his barrister, the prosecutor and the judge wove a special kind of magic – a triangle of dialogue peppered with mysterious numbers and references. A second lawyer, female, sat next to Justin's barrister – 'They thought it would be good for the jury to see a woman on the defence team,' Justin confided to me later. Solicitors also sat with the barristers – for the Crown, one with long auburn hair and a Mona Lisa smile. Busy scribbling notes and flicking through files to fish out documents, the solicitors did much of the legal grunt work, their notes fuelling the orators in the magic triangle. Justin's mother, a largish strong-looking woman with a blonde bob and wearing a blouse and brooch, sat behind his lawyer. His younger brother was also there, wearing a black suit, and so too a young woman I later found out was Justin's girlfriend.

Frowning in concentration, they cocked their heads as they tried to snatch at fleeting fragments of clarity. 'You can't isolate 200 from 201,' said one lawyer. 'It flows from 199.' The three men in the triangle were trying to untangle the events on the evening of Collingwood's premiership win. How to separate whatever occurred between Justin and Sarah in an alleyway from the incident in the bedroom of the South Melbourne townhouse? How to stem the flow of the bedroom narrative into the alleyway? Where did the narrative of the trial begin, how did it end, and what to do with the middle? How to question witnesses without them slipping up and revealing to jurors that there was more to the night than a solitary rape complaint?

It was a strange thing to watch. It was as if the defence counsel, the prosecutor and the judge were getting their story straight before presenting it to the jury. I couldn't quite go along with them. How could they unravel the sequence of events without losing the complexity of what was being assessed? Or was that the point – to keep it simple for a jury? Were they hollowing out the truth by excising a part of the night, or making the truth sharper, easier to see?

'... 303 Dorcas Street, a place which I do not wish to go,' said Chris Ryan SC, the Crown prosecutor, referring to the events in the bedroom. Judge Mark Taft agreed, and so for the most part did defence counsel Thomas.

> JUDGE: It will ... mean that the forensic evidence may have
> no carriage ... I was quite unsure that admission of that
> evidence would do anything whatsoever except damage

forensically the accused and no doubt blacken the
complainant in the process.

PROSECUTOR: ... That may or may not be good enough, but
it was the way in which I intended to proceed with it
because so far as the complainant is concerned, on any
view of it, she was the subject of the most appalling of
conduct in that house.

JUDGE: Very ugly happenings.

PROSECUTOR: Indeed, and so far as Mr Dyer is concerned I
would have thought the last thing he would want would
be to have been the person in the room watching that,
because that allows me to do all manner of things to Mr
Dyer. So hence –

JUDGE: This would be a much more confined trial and have
less problematic issues attached to it if the issues were
narrowed ...

I looked at Justin to gauge how he felt about his memory of
the evening being erased and shrunk, but his face was devoid of
expression. His suit hung box-like over his stocky body. I thought
of Meursault, the protagonist in Albert Camus' *The Outsider*,
who said that he felt like an intruder at his own trial.

'I noticed that almost all the people in the courtroom were
greeting each other,' Meursault observed, 'exchanging remarks
and forming groups – behaving, in fact, as in a club where the
company of others of one's own tastes and standing makes one
feel at ease. That, no doubt, explained the odd impression I had
of being de trop here, a sort of gate-crasher.'

*

'If I could get my hands on that girl,' said Justin's mother, Carol, while we waited at the pedestrian lights outside the County Court. I had introduced myself in the morning break and now we were going for a coffee nearby.

'Do you know somewhere?' Carol asked me, being the only local among them. I didn't. I knew this only as the 'grey' part of town, where even the corresponding piece of sky above seemed to be permanently ashen. It was the city's legal district, and the stairs leading into the Magistrates' Court were blotted with smokers, bit player crims and media scrums, while lawyers, solicitors and barristers walked along the footpath, heads down and trailing black suitcases on wheels, or for those behind the times clutching at bloated manila folders. Their horsehair wigs and black cloaks blustered as the wind, forever trapped in these streets, whipped around them like a Chinese dragon.

We walked past Petty Sessions Café. I asked after Justin's father – having seen him at the committal. Carol looked at me tearfully. 'He's been diagnosed with cancer.'

'It's the stress,' said Justin's younger brother.

'The doctor says it's not stress,' said Carol.

'But it is stress,' finished Justin.

And Galbally, I enquired, what had happened to him?

Back in the courtroom, despite his absence, Galbally's handiwork had come up: the police had been told that the Collingwood players would not make a statement once it was recognised that they would not be the subjects of a prosecution.

Judge Taft, it seemed, had no time for the football lawyers' antics.

THOMAS: Obviously the issue as to whether the witness
    Beams is to be called is a very significant one … He is an
    eyewitness. He is a material witness and it's not just a
    question of credit.

TAFT: Yes … It may be that despite his reluctance he is
    going to have to give evidence as to that matter … I
    would hate to interrupt his training schedule but it may
    be necessary.

Beams, it appeared, had seen something that conflicted with
Sarah's statement, evidence that could be helpful to Justin's case.
But strangely, the defence was reluctant to call him as a witness,
perhaps afraid that the presence of the AFL footballer on Justin's
side of the court would be construed by a jury as 'footy mates'
sticking together, or wary of what a cross-examination of the star
player could reveal. In the end, though, Taft ordered that Beams
be sought to give evidence. With his spectacles studiously
perched on the end of his nose and a sense of fairness that cut
through the lawyers' strategising, Taft had an Atticus Finch air
about him.

Now, walking with the Dyer family, I learned that a month
before the trial, they had had to scramble for new lawyers after
receiving a bill that only a QC can send and only the likes of a
top football club can pay. Justin's parents sold their house to
raise funds and Carol went to work in a womenswear chain
store. Stunned, they weren't even sure how they had found themselves in this mess.

'Justin was told to go talk to Galbally, that he'd look after
him,' Carol said. 'We were so far away and didn't know anyone

in Melbourne, so when he told us he had a lawyer, we just went along with it.'

We found a café and sat down at a large table. On either side of me, Justin's younger brother and Carol were talkative, eager to chat about how upset they were and how unfair the charges were, each wanting to know what I thought. As I juggled their questions, I glanced at Justin, trying to get a sense of him. He was reserved, reticent. He felt very faraway, distant. He turned his head to talk to his girlfriend and I took in the back of his neck, the trim lines where a clipper had snipped at his dark, almost black, hair.

Later, when I met his older brother, I could see that Justin was the quiet one of his siblings, passive and content not to get a word in edgeways while the rest of his family filled the silence around him – the kind of child a mother might worry she is not giving enough attention to. 'He's never been in trouble,' exclaimed Carol. 'Of all my boys, he's the one I've worried least about.' In a family that loved their footy, Justin was their star. But as I watched him across the table, I sensed he might not have shone brightly enough. He had inherited his talent for the game from his father, who still went on footy trips with his mates, trips from which stories trickled down into family folklore, like the time one of them lay down on a golf course, holding a tee between his teeth while the team lined up to hit off.

Justin's girlfriend, Vanessa, sat with her hands in his and her green eyes constantly searching his face for signs of how he was coping. She had met him after the charges were laid. I instinctively raised an eyebrow at her and she smiled. 'I know, my friends think I'm crazy. But …' she trailed off, looking at him.

Now that Justin had moved back home to Queensland, the two spent as many weekends together as they could afford.

I told the family that I was writing about footy culture and the increasingly scrutinised off-field behaviour of footballers, and asked Justin if he thought the world of football had anything to do with the situation he was in.

Justin considered for a moment before answering. 'It's got me here, that's true, but it's also getting me through this.'

He explained that after Coburg dropped him from the state league, a regional team picked him up. At the end of the season he was awarded Best and Fairest, keeping his cool even as spectators sledged him. 'The whole season people were leaning over the railing yelling, "Rapist, they're gunna get you inside, pretty boy."' But his new team had embraced him, Justin said, and playing football was the only time when he stopped thinking about the rape charges.

Justin was good at football. Playing at top state level in Queensland, he was regularly noted as one of the best on ground, a talented midfielder, able to read the play and move the ball forward. I asked if he'd moved south two years ago with a couple of his teammates to see if they could get into the AFL. 'No,' he said. They'd just wanted to play footy 'somewhere different.'

Vanessa interrupted. 'That's not really true,' she said.

He looked at her and shrugged. 'Well, yeah, maybe there was a hope that we'd be noticed, but ...' He trailed off before finishing his sentence. 'But that won't happen now.'

I asked Justin how he felt about the decision to excise the bedroom events from his trial. He grimaced. 'It seems strange, sort of like lying, but my lawyer thinks it's better for me that it's not included. That it would reflect badly on me.'

In the morning's deliberations, the legal triangle had kept referring to an 'utterance' made by Justin that would have to be carved out. 'What are they talking about?' I asked him.

'It was a stupid off-the-cuff remark,' he said. 'After we left the alleyway, on the way to get a taxi, I'd said to her, "You're not going to tell the police Collingwood raped you, are you?" And she said, "No, of course not, I'm not that sort of girl." It was a dumb thing to say. I wish I'd never said it. But the next day, when I texted her, I asked if she was going to hold to her promise.'

The text, I found out later, had read, 'Hey, how you feeling this morning. Are you going to hold to your promise? LOL.'

The prosecution was going to link the text message to Justin's earlier 'utterance.' 'But it wasn't about that at all. She had promised me in the cab that she'd come over to my place that afternoon.'

'She slept with four others that night!' Carol cut in, looking at me for some kind of affirmation.

I kept my eyes on Justin. 'I don't know if that's accurate,' I replied, 'but even if it is, I think the issue is whether she consented to every person that night.'

A confused silence fell over the table, until Vanessa said, 'Well, she doesn't seem that traumatised,' explaining that she'd seen Sarah out nightclubbing a few times.

'People react in different ways,' I said, and thought again of Meursault, whose trial became less about the murder he had committed than about his improper response to his mother's recent death. (He went swimming with a girl and to the movies after the funeral.)

Ironically, though, it was Justin who had reacted in the way that people might have expected of Sarah. Since the police investigation, he hadn't been to clubs or parties, and for the most part didn't go out at night except to a mate's place. Even then he was not always at ease. Carol confided in a low voice that they had been really worried about him, but, 'Things improved since he met Vanessa.'

Everyone beamed at Vanessa – 'She's been wonderful.' I liked Vanessa. But it was also clear that in the eyes of this family she was a 'good girl,' not like the liar who had gotten Justin into this mess. I was growing aware that, at this table, there were 'types' of women. Not sure how to take Carol's attention, Vanessa laughed, shyly moving closer to Justin.

As we walked back to court, the hot dry wind tailed us. It was February and summer clung to the city. On the footpath, people stuck to the cool strips of shade alongside the tall grey buildings. Walking together, the Dyer family looked strong. But as Carol kept checking her phone for chemo updates and Justin tried not to think about the debt his family was in, I could see the chinks. I was reminded of footballers who, in spite of their injuries, play on, looking like beige mummies, their bodies held together with Elastoplast strapping.

Taking our seats in the courtroom, I watched as the Dyer family moved to sit on the far left of the room and Justin went back to the dock. I looked at the empty seats behind the prosecution and had no one with whom to compare the Dyer family's suffering.

At the committal hearing, Sarah had given her evidence in closed court, as she would during the trial. The room was cleared except for the magistrate, lawyers, Justin and his parents, who sought permission to sit in, as long as they sat out of the camera's view.

*

Later I found some of Sarah's photos on the internet. They were of her and her friends in their final year at an all-girls high school. The photos made me smile and reminded me of my own four years at a girls-only school – something I had never fully appreciated until now. The friendships and constant hugging, all over each other like puppies, the jokes that weren't funny which made us laugh even harder. Even the viciousness of girls that I'd experienced in a previous co-educational school seemed less prevalent. The girls in the photos were pulling faces, mucking around, dressing up for laughs. In one photo, four girls grinned as they posed comically in some seriously garish tracksuits.

The smiles were genuine, faces healthy, sun-kissed and pink-cheeked. There was no pouting, unless it was in jest, no make-up, no 'tilt your head down, then look up with your eyes' modelling moves for the camera. I remembered running around, brown legs always bruised from sport poking out of a school dress. I remembered not thinking. Not in a careless way, but in a way that I now realised was free of being watched, of being appraised.

Sarah was lovely. She was tall with a sprinkle of light freckles across her nose, pale-skinned, with small white teeth, sandy long hair and blue eyes. Her arms were draped around her friends. In one picture, in sports uniform, she hugged two girlfriends and they all looked relaxed, incredibly young and honest. In another photo, she was caught mid-movement, her hand confidently on her hip, lips clamped shut in a stifled grin, a picture of fun and sass. At the end-of-school shenanigans Sarah had dressed in fake leopard-print fur, her hand curled like a claw in the air, and you could almost hear her growl like a cat before dissolving into laughter.

Sarah already looked older than her friends. Not quite fully engaged in the wildness, the innocent freedom of her peers, she had a touch more confidence and wariness. It was her beauty, that's for sure. She was more than that, I found out – an athlete, a leader at school, with a final-year result that put her in the top 5 per cent of the state – but it can be beauty that brings a separation from a flock of girlfriends, that forces a young woman to be that little bit more self-aware; a power, yes, something that unlocks doors to rooms you're not sure you want, or are ready, to enter.

# CHAPTER 4

On 30 September 2012, tens of thousands of people marched down Sydney Road, in Melbourne's inner northern suburbs, to honour Jill Meagher, a 29-year-old woman who had disappeared a week earlier. Holding placards calling for unity and an end to violence against women, the solemn crowd stretched for over a kilometre along the busy street, swelling around trams and breathing in the sweet syrupy smell of baklava and hookah pipe cafés. Just two days before the march, her body had been found in a shallow grave in country Victoria – she had been raped and murdered.

Outside a bridal shop, the marchers paused to lay flowers and tributes at the door. Here, CCTV footage had provided a crucial piece of the puzzle that led police to find Jill Meagher's body. The footage makes for eerie viewing. After visiting two local bars with friends, Meagher had opted to walk home by herself in the early hours of the morning. Her apartment was less than 800 metres away. In the surveillance footage, a lanky man in a blue hoodie, light denim jeans and white sneakers walks past the bridal shop. Then, less than a minute later, the same man doubles back. Another minute passes before he returns, this time talking to a woman, Jill Meagher. His body turns to the side as he walks, attempting to draw her into a conversation. Meagher stops, steps back and wavers a little on her heels, as if waiting for him to leave her alone and walk ahead. It's the last known image of her alive.

When Meagher's body was found, the journalists Chip Le Grand and Sophie Gosper wrote in the *Australian*:

Of all the possibilities that confronted police when Ms Meagher first went missing early last Saturday morning, this was the least likely; a genuinely random, opportunistic attack.

*Opportunistic*. It's the same word that haunted me when watching the footage – and at Justin's trial. And no – it is not the same thing. Jill Meagher was raped and murdered, and it is unlikely that the trial arising out of her killing will revolve around establishing whether she consented or not. And yet the word lingers in my mouth. Opportunistic. To exploit a chance offered by immediate circumstances, without a general plan or moral principle.

\*

'Guilty is guilty,' the policeman had said. But the Dyer family felt a great injustice had been done to their son. In a month the trial would provide a verdict on what had happened in the alley that night, but if Justin was the fall guy, then the backstory needed to be understood. What had happened in the townhouse? Sarah Wesley was at the centre of numerous opportunistic manoeuvres on the night of the grand final, but was this because she was vulnerable? Or was she 'up for it'?

Repeatedly, to anyone who would listen, I relayed the vague details I'd gleaned about the night Sarah Wesley went home with Nate Cooper. She'd met him once before, I'd begin. They'd been messaging each other and caught up again at a nightclub. Around 4 a.m., the two walked back to his house, where some of his friends were sitting around and drinking, including his cousin and housemate, John McCarthy, and Dayne Beams, both Collingwood footballers. They were celebrating their grand final win. After saying hello, Sarah and Nate went to his bedroom. Then, when they were close to having sex, the door opened and a few of the other guys came in.

At this point, my listeners would shake their heads in horror. 'How could she even begin to consent to that?' said one friend. 'How'd she even have time to consider what she wanted?'

'But she could have, right?' I replied. 'I mean, people do go along with it. How else did these guys get it into their heads that it was okay?'

'Well, it sounds shithouse,' she said. When I added that the trial wasn't even about what had happened in the house, but in an alleyway afterwards, her disgust only deepened. 'You mean to say that this guy says she consented to having sex in an alley after that? How is it even possible to be mentally capable of saying "yes" after all that?'

'She could have ...' I said, trailing off, unnerved by my friend's conviction, and my lack of it. Then I remembered the policewoman at the committal. Sarah had told the police that she'd felt 'compelled' to have sex with Beams, but 'not forced.'

I passed that on to my friend, adding 'she'd felt duty-bound to go through with it.' I paused, then said tentatively, 'At what point does peer pressure become so threatening that it's rape?'

A little appalled, my friend looked me in the eye. 'Those men had all the power,' she said. 'She was in a strange house, in a bedroom with most of her clothes off, and a bunch of guys she does not know came in expecting to fuck her. I mean, did they even prepare themselves for the possibility of her saying no?'

\*

'There is definitely a pattern, an attitude across the whole game that was so sleazy and underhand and nasty. We heard stories – horror stories – most of them you couldn't get people to go on the record, enough evidence and verified to go to print,' Jacquelin Magnay told me. 'Most of the stories were of humiliation, of taking advantage of women, and also deceiving women.'

Never insiders, never initiated into the inner sanctum of football, female journalists were free to ask the questions that had been gathering dust for years. What broke things wide open was, in 2009, the ABC *Four Corners* episode 'Code of Silence,' an investigation into rugby league by the reporter Sarah Ferguson. Among a series of revealing incidents, the program revisited the pre-season tour taken by the Cronulla Sharks to New Zealand first publicised by Magnay and Halloran.

SARAH FERGUSON: In 2002, 19-year-old Clare, as we'll call her, was working part-time as a waitress at the Racecourse Hotel on the outskirts of Christchurch. After finishing

work Clare went with two of the players back to their
room. One of them started kissing her.

CLARE: I didn't want to, you know, make a big deal out of a
kiss and even though it was rough and disgusting and I
was a piece of meat even at that stage, but it was, you
know, it was, you know, it was nothing, it was just a kiss.

SARAH FERGUSON: Over the next two hours, at least twelve
players and staff came into the room. Six of them had sex
with Clare, the others watched. Five days after the event
Clare made a complaint to police.

Clare described to *Four Corners* how throughout the evening
there were always hands on her, flipping her over, rubbing penises
in her face, while others stood around masturbating. 'Every time
I looked up, there would be more and more people in the room
and, um, there's lots of guys in the room watching, ah, maybe
two or three that were on the bed that were doing stuff to me.'

CLARE: I only remember this whole time, I only remember
one player definitely, it was Matty Johns.

At this, *Four Corners* cut to footage of the Logie Awards showing
Matthew Johns, former Shark and now TV personality, accept an
award on behalf of the NRL's own version of *The Footy Show*. At
the time of the incident in Christchurch, he was thirty years old.

CLARE: He laughed and he joked and he was very loud and
boisterous and thought it was hilarious and, you know,
kept it going.

SARAH FERGUSON: Matthew Johns and fellow player Brett
Firman told *Four Corners* they were the first players to
have sex with Clare. Firman said 'she was up for it a
hundred per cent.' Johns denies he kept it going, saying
when he had finished he 'took a step back.'

CLARE: They never spoke to me, they spoke just to themselves, among themselves, laughing and thinking it was
really funny. When you have sex with someone and it's
nice and you talk and you touch – and this was awful.
This was nothing like, nothing like that.

SARAH FERGUSON: Some players even came into the room
through the bathroom window.

CLARE: I had my eyes shut a lot of it and when I opened my
eyes, there was just a long line at the end of the bed.

SARAH FERGUSON: What was going through your mind
when this was happening?

CLARE: I thought that I was, that I was nothing. I thought
I was worthless and I thought I was nothing. And I
think I was in shock. I didn't scream and they used a lot
of like mental power over me and belittled me and
made me feel really small, like I was just a little old
woman.

SARAH FERGUSON: Towards the end Paul Gallen, the current
captain of the Cronulla Sharks, went in to see what was
happening. Gallen told us it was pretty much all over by
then, but nothing bad had happened anyway. After two
hours it ended.

CLARE: I think maybe one of the guys said she's had enough,
or something along those lines, like alright guys, let's wrap

it up, she's had enough. And so I put my clothes on and
walked out.

SARAH FERGUSON: Did anybody talk to you while you were
putting your clothes back on?

CLARE: No, no one. I was nothing.

SARAH FERGUSON: Afterwards in the car park, Matthew
Johns told *Four Corners*, he went up to Clare and said he
was sorry about the other guys coming into the room.

Clare went on to describe the downward spiral her life took
after the incident – drinking heavily, reclusive, suicidal and
cutting her wrists. She had even bought a rope to hang herself.
The policeman who investigated the allegations said he received
several distressed phone calls from her over the years.

Four weeks after the complaint was made, the police interviewed forty players and staff from Cronulla. As Ferguson
reported, 'In their graphic descriptions, those present said she
had consented to each and every act. No charges were laid.'

Warned about the content of the *Four Corners* program,
Matthew Johns made a pre-emptive apology on Channel 9's *The
Footy Show*. 'It's put my family through enormous anguish and
embarrassment, and for that, I'm just …' He shook his head as if
bewildered and tapped the table with his hand. 'Well, you can't
say sorry enough. But, ah, the police did investigate the situation
at the time, the allegation, and there were no charges laid.'

His co-host, Paul 'Fatty' Vautin, then leaned over, patted him
on the back and said, 'Alright, let's get on with the show.'

*

The apology failed to anticipate, let alone fathom, the scale of public response that would follow the *Four Corners* revelations. Outrage was palpable throughout the nation. Pressure mounted on Channel 9 as sponsors began to withdraw support from the Sharks, the club losing almost a million dollars in annual funding. After 'monitoring the situation' for a week, Channel 9 decided to 'stand down' Johns from the network indefinitely, as did the Melbourne Storm rugby team, which had him as an assistant coach. (The banishment, however, was short-lived. When the 'fuss' died down, Channel 9 tried to woo Johns back with a contract worth more than he'd originally been paid, but he declined and signed on with a rival network for *The Matty Johns Show*.)

The NRL was quicker to react. An hour after 'Code of Silence' aired, David Gallop apologised on behalf of the game for the 'appalling' and 'unacceptable' behaviour of some players towards women. At a press conference a day later, he advised players that such sexual activity was degrading to women and warned that those who took part in it could be kicked out of the game. 'If you are not on board with the change that we are endeavouring to implement, then don't play rugby league.'

Some players didn't agree. A senior NRL player spoke on condition of anonymity to the *Sydney Morning Herald*'s Jamie Pandaram.

It's fine for David Gallop to come out and say you can't have group sex, but the last thing blokes will be thinking about on a Friday night at the club is David Gallop. I don't know how a chief executive can come out and say we can't have group sex if it's consensual. It's like discrimination because that is a person's private life. It's like saying you can't be homosexual, or you can't have such-and-such sexual preferences. How can he tell us what we can do in our private lives? What if there's more women than guys – is that wrong, too?

The reality is that these incidents don't tend to involve more females than males. It is usually a lone woman with three or more men. And while the act is nothing new – the former coach and sports writer Roy Masters says it has been an unofficial team-bonding activity for some time – it's only recently that players have been forced to defend it, and part of that defence is calling it 'group sex.' But off the record, among coaches and footballers, it's always been a 'gangbang.'

The anonymous player continued his lament:

We already have so many rules; we can't drink on these days, we can't go to these places, now we can't have group sex. About the only thing we can do these days is go to club functions and just hang around other players. That's just isolating us more from the rest of the world, and it could lead to even more violent acts.

The league's adviser on gender issues, Catharine Lumby, agreed that players' lives were already subject to endless rules. 'People say, "All these guys need is a boot camp" – that kind of thing. But these men are already over-trained. They need to learn to think for themselves.'

She put emphasis on educating players about seeking 'informed and continued' consent, a position that saw her lambasted by the media. '[According to Lumby] if this teenager consented to group sex, there was nothing more for Johns and his mates to know,' wrote the *Herald Sun* columnist Andrew Bolt sarcastically. 'Indeed, none seemed to think they had a duty to protect this young woman from what degraded them all. She agreed. End of questions.'

Bolt wrote equally scathingly of Lumby and the NRL's Playing by the Rules education program. In his eyes, it was nothing more than a 'sensitivity course designed by the hippest postmodern feminists.' The program 'trilled' that 'players were unequivocal that sexual assault of women is always wrong,' although 'a majority of players want ongoing education about how to negotiate sexual encounters in a way which ensures informed consent is always obtained.'

> No surprise that boys want to learn how to make a girl always say 'yes.' But the real challenge is how to make them listen when she says 'no' ... I've long thought a big stick helps a bozo to hear better, but Lumby's report is a model of faddish thinking on crime and punishment, relying on two fatal notions: that we can reason anyone out of being a bastard, and can trust him to 'negotiate' their morality.

Next to put the boot in was Miranda Devine writing in the *Sydney Morning Herald*:

> Who could blame the players for being confused? Lumby emphasises 'consent' ... But emphasising a legalistic notion of consent, without moral context or any expectation of women to modify their behaviour, leaves players unmoored from the

real consequences of their behaviour. It is putting an unsustainable pressure on the ability of young footballers, perhaps drunk, insensitive, or carried away by group dynamics, to discern the subtleties.

Devine initially put the responsibility on Matthew Johns for the New Zealand incident:

Plenty of young women are neither assertive nor articulate enough to stand up to charismatic older football stars. Johns was thirty at the time, and married. He knew better.

But ultimately she laid the blame at the feet of feminism:

It is unfair to expect men to bear full responsibility for sexual mores as the boundaries of acceptable practice are blurred. Young women are told they can act and dress any way they please, and it is men, alone, with their supposedly filthy, uncontrollable sexual desires, who must restrain themselves … There is no understanding that female sexual attitudes have always been the most successful regulator of male sexuality – not politically correct re-education programs that are exercises in legal risk management for the NRL.

This is, of course, where the 'uh-oh' comes in. The suggestion that women are the regulators and ultimately the suppressors of men's sexual behaviour returns us to the premise that violence against women is a women's issue, a corollary of which is that if a woman seeks sex as a man might, then she invites potential violence and mistreatment. For his part, Bolt seems close to proposing a little 'do's and don'ts' sex handbook when he writes that trusting people to negotiate consent instead of providing hard-and-fast rules assumes 'that people are smart enough and strong enough to work out all by their uncertain selves what's good for them.' Such a handbook, likely to be penned by him, would certainly diminish all of our sex lives.

But Bolt does have a point. As Sarah Ferguson said:

> *Four Corners* doesn't say that what took place in room 21 of the Racecourse Hotel was sexual assault. But a woman involved in degrading group sex can still be traumatised whether she consents or not.

If mere consent can result in a ten-person gangbang with a lone teenage girl at its centre, then what good is it? How to ascertain the calibre of someone's consent? For all the good intentions of the feminist slogan 'no means no,' the resulting awareness has been too simplified and the true meaning of consent has fallen by the wayside. After all, by the logic of 'no means no,' surely 'yes means yes'? But people agree to do things all the time without an understanding of what they are undertaking. True consent relies on three factors: a capacity to say yes, a knowledge of what exactly one is saying yes to, and that the decision to say yes is an independent one, free of threat.

And so Catharine Lumby's urging of NRL players to seek continued and informed consent in 'high-risk scenarios' such as group sex is good advice, except for one thing: it negates the entire point of a gangbang. The reality is that a gangbang is not group sex, and the difference is in the *tone* of the act. Group sex implies that multiple participants are mutually engaged with one another and that is perhaps way too gay a concept for footballers. Gangbangs, on the other hand, tend to focus on a central person. Most, if not all, sexual acts are performed on this person.

Then there's the terminology of a gangbang – for example, the 'club bun' (she's the bun, the players are the meat and are to 'put it in' any way they can), or roasting a pig on a spit (she's the meat, the players are the skewer). And if a woman is considered nothing more than meat, then what capacity for consent can she possibly have? What in-depth inner life can she have? Who would think to ask a piece of meat for *true* consent? Gangbangs are about sex, yes, but they're also about 'being with the boys' – the woman involved is no more than a 'vehicle for bonding,' as Roy Masters put it.

Masters wrote that players enjoy each other's company and 'anything that unites them,' listing excursions such as fishing, going to the movies and paintball, before adding gangbangs (although he calls it group sex) to the mix.

Okay, such relatively innocent outings are a far cry from group sex, but sexual satisfaction isn't the aim of this sleazy exercise, during which the guys laugh at the sexually incompetent – the ones who are flaccid or, more particularly, the ones rejected by the girl because they are ugly or awarded a mark of one out of ten by her for their lack of sexual prowess. The sex isn't equalising; rather it's the intimacy within the tribe, being 'one of the boys,' which is the bonding mechanism.

Despite all the teasing from commentators that players involved in 'club buns' obviously just want to fuck one another, the act is aggressively heterosexual, a badge of masculinity.

Ian Roberts was the first professional rugby footballer in the world to come out to the public as gay. Talking to the *Sunday Telegraph*'s Claire Harvey, he said that 'group sex' encounters such as those with the Bulldogs in Coffs Harbour struck him as 'not in any way homoerotic.'

> I've got no problem with group sex if everyone's open-minded and respectful. I'm a gay man, my God, I'm totally aware it happens, but the idea of one poor girl on her own there in that situation – it's totally disempowering.

In fact, moments after Matthew Johns's apology on *The Footy Show*, with Fatty saying 'Let's get on with the show,' they launched into a comedy skit about 'the other Johns brother,' the brother no one spoke of when it came to the league's famous family. His name was Elton, Elton John*s* – get it? Matthew Johns played Elton, wearing a blond wig and big glasses, and was dragged to the hospital by his father, Gary Johns, also a former player, who pulled him up to the triage desk and said, 'I want to return this. It's faulty.'

Andrew Johns, Matthew's younger brother – 'the world's best rugby player,' according to some commentators – made an appearance (a real family event this skit, just minutes after Johns had apologised for the distress and embarrassment he had caused his family). 'Like Dad,' Andrew joked, 'I'm so ashamed of him.' And then, just in case viewers didn't get it, there was this. Still playing Elton, Matthew Johns said to the camera, 'Dad only knew I was gay when he walked in on me and my boyfriend Ian.'

'You dated Ian Roberts?' asked the reporter.

Ian Roberts was sitting at home watching that night. He later told Claire Harvey that he'd tuned into *The Footy Show* to see what Johns would say in his apology and was disappointed that the apology focused mainly on the pain of his wife and family. The subsequent skit was too much for Roberts:

> Guys, what you don't understand – you think it's funny, but there are gay kids in the suburbs who are killing themselves because they don't know what to do about their sexuality. They kill themselves. This poor girl has spoken about suicide. This is not a joke anymore.

\*

'I never got the sense it was gay,' said Tony Wilson, a writer who was briefly drafted for Hawthorn Football Club in the early nineties. He recalled fellow players throughout his footy career stroking his chest in the locker room or faking anal sex whenever anyone bent over. 'It was more attention-seeking and juvenile. It was fucking annoying.'

It was footy players' humour.

Another former AFL player told me about a similar brand of comedy after his team had played a match. 'I was laying on a bench being massaged by this big ugly brute of a guy, my eyes closed and mouth hanging open and ———, on his way to the shower, rammed his penis into my mouth, then ran away.'

When I told some male friends about this 'gag,' a few responded angrily. 'Those bastards,' said one. 'You know, all your school life, those footy jocks practically patrolled the yard and whether you were gay or not, you had to make sure you never slipped up, did something that could be seen as gay, otherwise these bastards would make your life hell. Then you hear something like this, I mean *fuck them*.'

But I can't help wondering – despite how it *looks* – if these kinds of pranks, jokes and even gangbangs are a form of surveillance in themselves.

One of the reasons – I think – that so many people watch football is not just for the athleticism and the biffo, but also for the tenderness. The sheer unadulterated joy when someone scores, the meshing of happiness, the hugging, and players helping haul one another off the grass, sometimes roughing up a player's hair once his feet are back on the ground. It is one of the most beautiful things about the game.

But is there a price players feel they must pay for this unchecked joy in one another? A point they have to prove to one another over and over?

# CHAPTER 5

Of the 800 AFL players, on average seventy-five are plucked from a draft of 1000 young men each year. At Collingwood Football Club annual general meetings, new draftees are introduced to the members. Eddie McGuire, a former CEO of the Nine Network and the Magpies' president, reads out their names, followed by height, weight and sprint speed. Lined up like top-quality cattle, they are the club's latest investments. Each has passed the closest thing to a quality assurance test to get there. An assortment of fitness tests, medical examinations, potential injury analyses, family background and psychology checks has occurred; their drop punt kicks have been filmed and studied in slow motion.

A final touch for the draftees is a photograph. Each potential recruit is to stare in steely fashion into the camera lens. They are coaxed to flex their muscles. Often a player will grip a red leather ball with one hand (handspan is also measured). This photo is perhaps the first inkling that these players are entering into more than a contract to play ball. The flash of the camera is as searing as a brand. Some players, stars in their country towns and schoolyards, are already naturals at fielding this kind of attention. But if you look closely at these early images, you may still glimpse the ghost of a boy, not yet rendered invisible by pounds of meat and muscle.

Although on the verge of adulthood, these footballers are about to enter a state of prolonged adolescence. For most of their peers, the social world is set to expand, but for these select few their already insular existence has just contracted. They will be expected to live, eat and train with their team, as if part of a single organism.

Young draftees are subject to diets, curfews, lectures and punishments, all of which sit awkwardly alongside storytelling nights where footballers initiate them into a clique of in-jokes, nicknames, bets and dares, where humour and humiliation control the power dynamic and veterans wax lyrical about the debauched adventures of Thommo, Johnno and Stevo.

Distil all that and transfer it into the body of a young man – this conflicting state of entitlement and responsibility – and you may well have a very confused soul.

Recruiters have already scoured the draftees' personal lives for distractions, hidden vices and interests that may later demand priority over the game. Supportive families are great, clingy ones not so good. In 1993, when the American professional footballer David Williams opted to miss a game after his wife went into labour with their first child, his club, the Houston Oilers, fined him and deducted over $100,000 from his pay. The club owner criticised him for his 'misplaced priorities.' Australian football codes demand a similar allegiance.

The former player Brent Crosswell, who was recently inducted as an 'icon' in the Tasmanian Football Hall of Fame

– 'they've upgraded me from "legend" status,' he told me, bemused – played much of his career under the highly respected coach Ron Barassi. 'He didn't like women getting in the way,' Crosswell recalled. 'Let's face it, women could be a bit at odds with sending a man back out on the field with an injury.'

'I remember one time, a fellow player's wife came to watch him play, she was heavily pregnant, and Barassi slammed him later in the change room, saying he was under the thumb and that she was distracting.'

In Kevin Sheedy and Carolyn Brown's book *Football's Women: The Forgotten Heroes*, they recount a footballer's wife's memory from the fifties of being hauled into her husband's club after recently giving birth to their first child. The coach interrogated her concerning her husband's feeble on-field performance, saying that he needed 'uninterrupted sleep' before games. Mortified, the wife promised the coach that her husband would not be disturbed by their baby.

Another former AFL footballer, Tim Watson, once wrote in the *Age* defending a Carlton player's decision to play footy instead of attending his brother's wedding:

> You can say to your brother: 'I will do my best to attend your wedding but if, by chance, we make the final of the Wizard Cup, my priority has to be to play for Carlton. I am a professional football player; it is an occupation I get well paid for and I have sworn an allegiance to the playing group that I am a part of whatever it is we do as a group.'

The same player's allegiance to his football 'family' was curiously reciprocated that year at the post-Brownlow Medal party at Crown Casino, where it was reported someone had slipped a Rohypnol into his long-term girlfriend's drink. This, by all accounts, was a 'prank' played on the player through the medium of his girlfriend.

*

'The way to improve relations between men and women is to expose the codes that control relations among men,' wrote John Stoltenberg, a feminist activist and author, in 1993. One such code among contact-heavy team sports is 'sledging,' or 'just a bit of banter,' as supporters like to refer to it. It involves getting in the ear of the opposition and baiting them – often sinking to *you're a faggot, a girl, a monkey, a black bastard* – so as to make a player see red and stuff up their game.

In 2008, an AFL footballer was sledged about his critically ill child, while the year before, two players exchanged punches after the West Coast Eagles' Adam Selwood pointed to a tattoo on his opponent's arm and reportedly said, 'I fucked her last night … Yeah, she's a slut.' The tattoo was a portrait of the player's six-year-old daughter. Selwood later told reporters that he didn't realise the tattoo was an image of the player's young daughter. 'I just saw it was a female,' he said.

The AFL tribunal cleared Selwood of insulting language – largely because his remarks were based on a misunderstanding. In other words, he'd just thought the picture was of a female, so no harm intended.

In the NRL, when Olsen Filipaina joined the Balmain Tigers in the eighties, he was one of the few Polynesians in the game.

'The way people treated me was unbelievable,' Filipaina told the *Rugby League Week* magazine some twenty years later. He recalled his own teammates deliberately trying to put him out of action in training sessions. During games, beer cans were thrown at him. 'I was called a black bastard, a nigger … it ruined rugby league for me.'

Spectators like to join in the sledging, female fans included, calling players 'girls' and 'poofters' when they duck out of a headlong crash, making monkey sounds when a black player gets the ball, or in the case of former NRL player Hazem el Masri, a champion goal-kicker for the Bulldogs and a devout Muslim, yelling 'fucking terrorist' and 'go home.'

Until recently, this was seen as part of the game, the challenge being to play harder and rise above the sledge. But such slurs are now being reported in the media, pressuring the codes to condemn the practice, all of which is raising the hackles of old-school footy insiders, men who say *get over it, princess*. The challenge now for the AFL and NRL is getting players to report controversial taunts, thus uprooting the code of 'what happens on the field stays on the field.' In other words: 'Don't dob.'

In the *Age* in 1986, Brent Crosswell recalled his club counselling him on what to say to the tribunal when his teammate was accused of making 'some extremely unpleasant remarks' to a goal umpire. Close by, Crosswell had heard what was said and was called on to give evidence.

His club coached him on what to say. 'Go away, you silly old moo,' recited Crosswell when the jury asked him what his teammate had said. 'The mouth of an ex-player on the tribunal dropped considerably,' wrote Crosswell, 'and the general assessment of the comment was not helped by some idiot chuckling in the press gallery.'

But times are changing, albeit with the usual dragging of feet. In 2011, West Coast became the AFL's first team to suspend one of its own players, Patrick McGinnity, after he told his opponent that he was going to rape his mother. The rival player, Ricky Petterd, reported the incident to the umpire, who then took it to the tribunal. The AFL applauded Petterd for speaking up, but McGinnity's manager, David Sierakowski – a former player whose father was a premiership player in both Aussie Rules and rugby league – said Petterd was thin-skinned: 'To have a Melbourne player come out and do this to him [McGinnity] is quite embarrassing.'

Less than a year later, the Port Adelaide midfielder Danyle Pearce reported Will Minson, a Western Bulldogs player, for a similar sledge. According to Pearce, Minson's comments implied raping his mother, including a line about pinning down her arms.

Fined and suspended by his club, Minson apologised publicly, while Pearce's family rallied around him, his father telling journalists he was pleased his son had made an official complaint, rather than leaving it on the field. 'Someone has insulted his family and he's standing his ground – I'm very proud of him,' he said.

Family was suddenly taking priority over the footballers' code of silence.

It was 1998 when the NRL first took action against racial vilification. Anthony Mundine reported Bulldogs forward

Barry Ward for calling him a 'black cunt.' The league fined Ward, but it took eight years for another player to come forward with a similar report. Then the South Sydney Rabbitohs stripped Bryan Fletcher of his captaincy after he called Parramatta's Dean Widders a 'black cunt' during a game. The club also took him off the playing list for a game and fined him $10,000.

Later, speaking to the Australian Human Rights Commission, Widders saw taking a stand as essential to players understanding one another better.

> I remember being at a function where two players who had played in the same team for over ten years were part of a general discussion. The non-Aboriginal player turned to the Aboriginal player and said, 'It's like when I used to call you a black so-and-so. You knew it was a joke.'
>
> The Aboriginal player, who has accepted this for years, finally had the courage to say, 'No, I didn't.'

The courage was contagious. In 2010, Timana Tahu – of Aboriginal and Maori heritage – walked out of the NSW State of Origin camp after the assistant coach, Andrew Johns, called an indigenous player on an opposing team a 'black cunt' at a team bonding session in a pub.

'You must shut that black cunt down,' Johns told the team's centre.

Tahu told relatives, 'He [Johns] has been using this term since I was eighteen. I can no longer look him in the eye.'

And despite an attempt to cover up the slur – team management had initially told officials that Tahu had left because of a hamstring complaint – anger from the public flared. Johns, a highly influential figure in the game, soon announced his resignation and days later was 'spotted' guest coaching an Under 15 boys rugby league team, a predominantly indigenous side.

Curiously, even those on the sidelines are now being taken to task. In June last year, 43,000 people gathered to watch Collingwood and Gold Coast on Sunday afternoon. Two rival players were tussling over the ball in the pocket when it went out of bounds. They were about to make their way back to the game when a Collingwood spectator started making monkey sounds and hurling racist abuse at Joel Wilkinson, a Gold Coast player of Nigerian descent.

Later on Nova radio, the other player, Collingwood's Dale Thomas, recounted their reaction. 'We were both a little bit shocked … We heard it and looked at each other, then I kind of looked back and shook my head at the area … where it came from.'

After the game, Thomas approached Wilkinson and said he would support him in whatever action he wanted to take. From there, Thomas lodged an official complaint, prompting his club to take action against the racist fan. After much sleuthing, the fan was identified and the Collingwood Magpies tore up his twenty-year membership.

It was a beautiful moment – a kindling of hope after what had seemed an endless round of bad media stories. Not only were two rival players *not* sledging each other, but they had taken a combined stand against a hateful spectator.

And yet, on-field sledging has also taken an unforeseen turn. With the introduction of the new moral codes, players are now getting sledged about their falls from grace. In 2008 St Kilda's Nick Riewoldt was overheard on an umpire's microphone saying to the Essendon player Andrew Lovett, 'You bash your fucking missus.' Lovett had just been fined $500 after breaching a restraining order. Less than a year later, Lovett was traded to the Saints.

Then there was Stephen Milne, one of the most notorious on-field sledgers. After the allegations of rape in 2004, many thought the serial pest got his comeuppance. Milne was called a rapist by rival players and booed by spectators. (Although, in a bizarre twist, some of his females fans started calling, 'Rape me, Milney! Rape me!') Even the highly respected Collingwood coach Mick Malthouse lost his cool and called Milne a 'fucking rapist' during a quarter-time break.

Milne told the *Age* in 2011 that he uses the abuse as motivation: 'It always happens and it always will. I don't think you'll ever be able to stop it. I love the sledge as well. There's a line you cross. I've crossed it once or twice, but blokes who cross it regularly probably should look at stopping.'

'Abuse as motivation' – sadistic though it sounds, I can understand it. I play basketball, and in my league there is one team we dread playing. They're okay players, above average in our grade, but it's not that we're worried about. It's how they play – immediately getting in our ears, holding the backs of our tops, and slugging under the ribs when the refs aren't looking. They make our blood boil, but even though I hate these games, I have to admit that I play some of my best basketball against them. I use the anger to drive over them with the ball, to lose them. There is no way, I think, I can let these bitches win. And for the most part, we don't. At the end of a game, there's relief when we've beaten them, as though we've won not just a game, but a battle against evil. But it's not fun. There are no handshakes, just residual anger.

In professional football, none of these creative spins on sledging the likes of Milne appear to involve moral judgments – rather they simply target perceived weak spots. And often, when players are caught out, many claim that their verbal slip-up occurred in the 'heat of the moment.' As Gideon Haigh pointed out in the *Age*, such a defence often falls flat. Concerning the 'I'll rape your mother' sledge, Haigh wrote:

What was almost as repellent as the words that West Coast Eagle Patrick McGinnity used in trying to intimidate Melbourne's Ricky Petterd at Etihad Stadium on Sunday was the expression on his face as he prolonged the exchange. Check the replay. He's pleased with himself. He positively leers. Having provoked a reaction, he goes back for more.

While it is tempting to take these sledges as instances of football's unique sexism and racism, sledging is less about what's said than a broader culture of bullying. Wrote Haigh:

Confronted by the mentality of 'whatever it takes' … it's hard not to feel a discomfiture about how players are encouraged to think of themselves and others.

\*

Four years ago, seven North Melbourne footballers put together a four-minute video showing the adventures of Boris – a condom-clad rubber chicken who liked to penetrate a frozen chicken carcass. Posted on YouTube, the video quickly caused a ruckus, with the players made to stand in front of journalists and hang their heads in shame. The video saw Boris and his presumably female chicken acquaintance getting it on in the supermarket, on a staff member's desk and in a player's locker. In one clip the two characters visit the pub for a beer and white wine before fucking in the toilet.

Two of the Kangaroos' senior players took the blame for being ringleaders, thereby revealing a serious case of prolonged adolescence – one of them was married with three children. For the most part, the video was plain stupid. Neither Boris nor the frozen chicken came out looking particularly fresh.

But one scene, in particular, raised the ire of onlookers. It showed the frozen chicken carcass being hurled into a wall and run over by a van before the rubber chicken returned to penetrate it. Boris just didn't know when to stop.

\*

Brent Crosswell once wrote a reminiscence of Vinny Catoggio, a player with a 'gentleness and pureness of heart,' a 'rather odd figure to find in football.' The young player was loved and celebrated by teammates, club officials and the media – at least he was until he put in a dismal grand final performance in 1973. 'He was a delightful player to watch, and he loved playing football,' wrote Crosswell, 'but after 1973 he was always struggling for a game.'

'It was the worst moment of my life,' Vinny told Crosswell. 'I was so upset and ashamed that I didn't want to look up. In fact I remember a committeeman coming along the lockers patting blokes on their heads. "Well done ... Hard luck," he was saying, but when he got to me he stopped, hesitated, and then moved on and patted the next bloke ... that really hurt me so much.'

On the day, Crosswell tried to console Catoggio in the locker room, saying it was 'just a bloody game' and recounting his own run-in with the fickleness of love lost after his own poor performance in a grand final. 'When I came into the rooms at half-time,' said Crosswell, 'Serge Silvagni, a player I admired, yelled, "You weak bastard," and threw an orange that splattered down the side of my face.'

As Crosswell pointed out, every footballer is only as good as his last game, and that insecurity can inform how they treat one another.

> Because of the pervasiveness of the sporting ethic that winning is everything and losing is nothing, in fact worse than nothing, immoral, Vinny and all those players who fail are made to feel unworthy, are 'shamed' ... Winning has become simply not losing but 'failing.' It seems an indictment of professional sport when the philosophy of winning is incompatible with the character of the Vinnys of this world.

And in this world of football, where winning and failing are the only two outcomes, it's not hard to see where *Schadenfreude* comes in. Winning not only requires a loser, but it can become tied up in the desire to see someone lose. They go down, you rise up.

Off-field, this *Schadenfreude* can become perverse. In a study of social and sexual relations between young men, the sociologist Michael Flood spoke to students at a military academy about their tight-knit male-only groups. He learned that a man who passes up on an outing with his mates to be with his girlfriend is called a 'WOM,' or 'Woman Over Mates' – in other words, pussy-whipped.

But the reverse term is perhaps more precise. Boys and men are being 'dick-whipped' by each other. Describing a culture of 'mateship built on sexism and homophobia, competitive banter, and an emphasis on stereotypically masculine exploits,' Flood pointed to a similar self-policing of such attitudes among male athletes and, in the United States, in college fraternities, where superiority is constantly reinforced and tested through sex, pranks, initiations and physical feats. Any threats, such as females, are fended off, while humiliating new members can bolster one's own ranking in a group.

But of course, this is just the top and bottom of the great macho 'stacks-on.' In the middle, somewhere in between the ringleaders and the unfortunate lambs, are the onlookers and spectators, neither winners nor losers, but the dick-whipped – the people who make this performance possible.

'When I told Vinny ... that football is "just a bloody game,"' Crosswell concluded, 'I wasn't telling him the truth.'

No, football isn't just a game. And some jokes just aren't funny.

# CHAPTER 6

In 2004, in the incident that prompted the AFL to consider the game's relations with women, the police questioned St Kilda's Stephen Milne over the alleged rape of a nineteen-year-old girl. At a pre-trial hearing, held a belated ten years after the incident, the court heard that Milne and another woman, and his teammate Leigh Montagna and the complainant, had consensual sex in separate rooms. Milne and his female partner then went into Montagna's darkened room. Milne and the complainant kissed, she believing he was Montagna. She claimed she called him 'Leigh' and repeatedly told him she did not want to have unprotected sex. On discovering it was Milne on top of her, the complainant ran out of the room into the bathroom. She cried, allegedly telling her friend, 'I thought it was Leigh, I thought it was Leigh. I kept saying no, but he kept putting it in.'

Scott Gladman, the detective who worked on the case, told *Nine News* that Montagna had sent the girl a text message the next day saying, 'I'm sorry' and 'We thought you knew.' But what would be the point of the prank if she knew? He also alleged that Milne sent a text to the girl's friend apologising for the 'mix-up.'*

Footballers love pranks. In fact, many of us do. Walking down a suburban street recently, I stopped mid-step as a dead rat tied to a piece of string dropped down from a tree in front of me. Looking up, I saw two boys hugging the tree branches and wobbling with suppressed laughter. The piece of string dangling from one of their hands was jiggling so hard that the rat looked like it was coming back to life. Not wanting to ruin the joke for them, I hid my smile and gave the rat a wide berth. A few metres away I turned and listened as the boys let out their gasps of laughter and the rat slowly jiggled its way back into the canopy.

I also remember watching footage of an AFL teammate hide under the bleachers after a training session and jump out, yelling 'Boo!' as Brendan Fevola walked past. The beautiful stupidity of it, the stunned look on Fevola's face and joy on his teammate's face as he pulled it off – I loved the boyish silliness of it.

A woman I interviewed told me about an AFL footballer who lived on her street and how one morning all the neighbours woke to find their wheelie bins had been arranged into a pyramid at the end of his driveway.

Some neighbours were grumpy – you know how precious people are about their bins – but I thought it was hilarious. His

---

* In late 2014 – ten years after the original complaint – Milne pleaded guilty to a lesser charge of social assault after the rape charges were dropped. A Victorian county court judge said that Milne's offending was 'out of character.' He went on to say that although Milne hadn't planned to offend, he had assaulted the victim after she had clearly said no. 'She did nothing wrong . . . she did not deserve what happened to her,' the judge said. Indecent assault carries a maximum sentence of ten years. Milne was fined $15,000.

teammates had blocked his car in the drive and the poor guy was scratching his head how to dismantle the pyramid without them all toppling down.

There can be an adorable childishness to pranks, a simplicity and an admirable 'I can't believe you're doing this' intense commitment. When I was young, I used to roam the streets with a gang of siblings and neighbours, making smoke bombs out of ping-pong balls, collecting dried dog poo and putting it in mixed lolly bags to give to unassuming kids, and, of course, knick-knocking. It was physical comedy, nothing cerebral about it, and it had an inexhaustible hilarity. But how do such silly, somewhat loveable pranks turn into spiking a drink with Rohypnol or bringing a girl back to a hotel room with five mates hiding in the bathroom?

*

'We used to have the Downlows,' recalled Craig Dermody, who played 'amateurs' in Gepps Cross, a rough part of Adelaide. The Downlows was Gepps Cross's equivalent of the AFL's Best & Fairest Brownlow Medal and it went to the local club member who did the most debauched thing on the end-of-season trip. The first Downlow that the then sixteen-year-old witnessed was at a seafood restaurant with the team and coach. 'The owner was getting drunk with us and our coach took the owner's tobacco pouch out of his front shirt pocket, pissed in it and put it back in the man's pocket.' Everything that could be drunk in the restaurant that night was drunk, said Dermody. The waitress – the owner's daughter – was screwed in the corridor. When I asked if they at least paid the bill, Dermody shook his head. 'Nah, the owner loved us. He wanted to be one of us.' For his 'pissing in the tobacco pouch' gag, the coach got the Downlow that year.

Another gag the Gepps Cross Rams liked was taking a piss while standing at the bar as the next round of pints was tallied up. When the St Kilda player Fraser Gehrig did the same thing in 2004 and pissed on the woman standing beside him, the media had a field day. Gehrig later claimed it was 'splashback' that had got her.

*

'You're not getting it, Anna,' said the former player Tony Wilson kindly, when I asked why pissing on a woman's leg at a bar was funny. 'It's comedy – this is their comedy. It is stunt-based, it's "Fuck, did you just see what so-and-so did?"'

When I asked Wilson about some of the antics he and his teammates got up to off the field, he rubbed his face as if still trying to gauge what expression he ought to have when talking about his playing days, a time in his life he loved, despite knowing, even then, that something was amiss.

'The vast majority of good times were non-sexual and non-nude. The most common prank was someone doing something to another's player's car, like filling it up with sawdust or hiding someone's bike.' Wilson paused. 'But in hindsight, I'd also argue that football is an abnormal society, and the off-field strangeness is very strange.

'In one team, in a huddle after a win, we had the Victory Chuckle which would then lead to the Victory Chopper, which involved one guy flipping out his dick. Or in the showers, you'd feel a splash of something warm on your leg and realise someone was pissing on you.'

Unofficial initiations were also part of joining a team. Wilson recalled the 'nude broom,' in which a younger player had to strip and run around with the broom whenever the senior players called out. When Wilson was the youngest player in his team, he was designated the 'Queen of Alcohol' at the end-of-season trip. 'I was stripped naked and then dressed in toilet paper and shaving cream. I had to deliver the alcohol to everyone. I would've looked funny and I'm not bearing the scars of that. But at the same time, it's odd and insular behaviour. It's not sexual, it's about humiliation and the older generation of "footballer" comedy.'

But then, said Wilson, there was the more serious stuff, instances where women were obviously being groomed.

'There were some deliberate creations of dangerous situations for females. One club I was at had the "Camel Night," which was a night where everyone was to get a hump. Each player and club official had to invite two girls who were not your girlfriend or wife and presumably not females you cared greatly for. So you had this party with no prying eyes, no one would get in trouble with their missus and tonnes of alcohol were supplied for these girls, who were basically nobody's responsibility.'

*

The sixties activist and prankster Abbie Hoffman once said that most pranks fell into one of three categories: satirical, vindictive and neutral – that is, soft on the stooge. In a *New York Times* article on the 'purpose of pranks,' the reporter Benedict Carey elaborated:

The bad ones involve vindictive skewering, or the sort of head-shaving, shivering-in-boxers fraternity hazing that the sociologist Erving Goffman described as 'degradation ceremonies.'

The 'satirical' prank often aims to reveal something about the joke's prey. Take as an example Hoffman's own stunt in 1967, when he and fellow hippies stood on a balcony overlooking the New York Stock Exchange and showered the floor with dollar bills. Stock traders famously knocked each other to the ground as they dove for the cash, the stunt bringing the tickertape to a halt for six minutes.

Similarly, vindictive pranks are revealing, but unbeknownst to the instigators, the revelation says more about the perpetrator than the victim. The *New York Times* quoted Jonathan Wynn, a sociologist at Smith College in Massachusetts, who believes pranks serve 'to maintain social boundaries in groups as various as police departments and sororities. And you gain status by being picked on in some ways. It can be a kind of flattery, if you're being brought in.'

Consider Sam Newman's response to public outrage at his mannequin gag about Caroline Wilson. He said it was a compliment of sorts, a sign that the *Footy Show* culture 'accepted' her. In other words, it wasn't really about Wilson, it was about *them*. About a subculture of men trying to find a place – albeit a very lowly place – in their world for a woman. Considering that it's all about the boys, the prey doesn't even need to be present. The photo of Wilson staple-gunned to a mannequin sufficed.

I remember one time, during my childhood exploits, when an older couple who lived in the old hat factory behind us, on whose door a gang of us repeatedly knick-knocked, stopped me on the street. I was on my own – the worst thing for a kid whose bravado relied on being surrounded by a mob of accomplices. In faltering English, they asked me, 'Why do you keep ringing our door? What have we done to you?' And I remember squirming, and saying, 'Nothing. You haven't done anything.' I couldn't understand why they thought they had to have done anything to be subjected to endless doorbell persecution. Why did they think it had anything to do with *them*?

And I wonder, how often does a woman realise this halfway through having sex with a footballer and then his mates when they get in on the action? Initially she is the subject of their attentions, they are all in on this together, but then, suddenly sobering, she realises she is not one of the guys, that all this, that guy who is taking pictures with his mobile phone, the other guy who has his pants down and is waiting his turn, has nothing much to do with her.

As a prank bonds its perpetrators and isolates its subject, does she realise that she really has nothing to do with what is happening around her, *to* her? And sure, it doesn't have to be a prank; possibly she knows how it looks on that guy's phone, that she was 'up for it.' And she was. She has no real recourse, only the slow dawning realisation that these guys, they don't really like her and maybe they never liked her. That this, this fucking, has nothing to do with her at all.

'We're not the "regrettable sex squad."' When I explained my confusion about a person's lack of recourse in such situations, this is what an ex-policeman told me his fellow officers often said. And perhaps they are right, it isn't a matter for the police, but I still wonder about the grey area, this gulf of uncertainty between consent and rape.

When we discussed this, Catharine Lumby nodded. 'Yes, there are many instances of behaviour that we found in our research into players' experiences that did not equate to sexual assault but are definitely extremely unethical behaviour – such as after having sex with a girl, throwing her out of your hotel room naked without her clothes for a joke. Or suddenly asking, "Do you mind if I invite my mate back?"'

As I scribbled Lumby's words into my notepad, I was reminded of a story I had heard from a young footballer about his time in the AFL. It wasn't the father-and-son day he and his dad attended, not knowing it was to be a beer-soaked event with strippers and one guy simulating sex with one of the ladies on a raised platform – he and his father tried not to look at each other for the entire day and never spoke of it afterwards. No, it was a story told to him by players about their end-of-season trip to the Gold Coast.

Four or five of the guys had gone back to a woman's house after meeting her at a club and had sex with her. At one stage, while she was occupied, a senior player shat in her shoe. The players who saw him grinned. When they were all gathering their clothes and things together later on, she offered them a lift back to their hotel. They accepted. She put her shoes on, foot straight in the shit.

And do you want to know the worst thing, went the punchline. She laughed with them, washed it off and drove 'the boys' home.

# PART 2
# THE GREY ZONE

# CHAPTER 7

'You can skin a cat a number of ways, Your Honour,' prosecutor Ryan said to Judge Taft. They were back on the subject of getting the Magpies' Dayne Beams to give evidence at Justin's trial in spite of his club's refusal.

The judge agreed. 'You can,' Taft replied, 'and whether it is a cat or a magpie may not be material.'

As the magic triangle continued to lay down the ground rules for the forthcoming trial, I gleaned snippets of the full story. The defence counsel, Malcolm Thomas, made the suggestion that Sarah's complaint against Justin was an afterthought. He read from Tom Shaw's police statement:

Then I asked how she got home. She said it was a $40 taxi ride from South Melbourne. 'Some guy put me in a taxi' and then somehow his name, Justin, came up.

'There is no complaint made at that stage,' said Thomas.
The judge wanted to know what Thomas was getting at.

'Do you want to cross-examine her about delayed complaint?' he asked. He reminded Thomas that if he was considering visiting what went on in the townhouse in front of a jury, he was entering risky territory.

Thomas nodded, countering that, 'If they [the Crown] want to be talking about being raped by a bunch of footy players, they themselves are introducing into evidence the sexual activities of the complainant.' But, he continued, he was only covering his bases. The defence had no desire to enter the bedroom of Dorcas Street, but he wanted to protect his client from any unforeseen arguments the prosecution might throw at them.

At this, prosecutor Ryan piped up. 'Can I be just a bit cautious and I may be out of court about this, but on the basis that I'm not leading with distress and on the basis I'm only leading the injury as to the knees, I don't want to be met with arguments at the end of the case that there was no distress. I just want to make sure. It has happened to me before, Your Honour.'

To an outsider, this was fascinating. It was like two enemies laying down the rules of engagement before going to war. And yet, it seemed to me that the true aspects of the war, the very reasons for going to war, were being smothered. By introducing the bedroom evidence, the court believed the charges being heard could be contaminated – but hadn't that already happened? Surely, whatever happened between Justin and Sarah in the alley had been precipitated by what happened in the townhouse?

As I watched Ryan and Thomas negotiate the trial's terms and conditions, I scribbled a note to myself: *listen to what's not being said*. It is an essential tenet of journalism, and as the night in question was being carved up, pieces of the puzzle removed and filed away, it had never been more pertinent. I realised that the jury members – when they were chosen – and I would be on vastly different trajectories: each of us would be seeking a truth, but these truths might well be at odds with each other, yet at the same time eerily similar. After all, the jury would have only two options, 'guilty' or 'not guilty' – a verdict of 'innocent' was not open to it. And I thought about Justin's family, their adamant belief that he had done no wrong: not only had he not raped Sarah, but he was wholly innocent. Was there no uneasy grey zone for them, no wondering what exactly Justin and his mates were doing that night? Was it just a case of their son picking up the wrong 'type' of girl? And Sarah – had she scrutinised her own actions, whether with perplexity, regret or rage? If a rape did not occur that night, then what had happened? Did she think a finding of rape would absolve her, and if so, for what did she want absolution?

The court was going to provide an answer at the end of Justin's trial – but not the answer to the question playing on my mind. How did it come to this?

*

'I was sitting in court listening to people's stories, having come from young people and adult [sex] offenders telling me in great detail what it was they did and how they did it and how they manipulated people,' said Patrick Tidmarsh to Nicole Brady of the *Age*. 'That was not being represented in court in a way that I understood, there was a bit missing.'

Tidmarsh had spent much of his career rehabilitating juvenile sex offenders and was now working with Victoria Police, training detectives in how to better understand and interview sex offenders about their crimes. 'The missing bit as Tidmarsh saw it,' wrote Brady, 'was not the specific details of the crime but all the events that led up to it.' The 'how' was vital, he explained, because often how victims react in a sexual assault can seem very strange to an outsider.

By omitting the events in the bedroom at Dorcas Street to avoid insinuations of promiscuity by the defence, what did the Crown have to work with? Ryan could not point to distress as a possible explanation for Sarah's behaviour with Justin. Nor could he refer to any forensic evidence – although, as Tidmarsh explained, more often than not forensic examinations after an alleged sexual assault show only that a sexual act had occurred.

Tidmarsh continued:

You'd think that if something happened to someone against their will, surely there would be evidence of that. But the explanation is … also because the person at that point co-operated, almost inevitably co-operated. To understand how and why they co-operated – submitted, complied, whatever word you use – you just can't understand that unless you have found out about the entire relationship up until that point, whether it was two minutes or two years.

Glenn Davies, the former head of Victoria's sexual crimes squad, agreed. 'It's important that a court hears how this attack took place, the details of how the relationship was cultivated,' he told me. But that, he believed, was not how most defence counsels wanted a rape trial to proceed – the less detail there was, the more likely this was to trigger a finding of reasonable doubt. 'The defence want the jury to be viewing it from afar, somewhere where they can just make out the movements and not hear what was said.'

According to Davies, 'Many judges will say that this detail is too prejudicial to the accused.' He threw up his hands. 'Too prejudicial? The entire prosecution is prejudicial!' That was the point, he implied. To expose the truth, all the details of an alleged assault must be aired. 'What about being prejudicial to the victim's prospects of justice – I mean, surely she deserves to have the truth come out?'

Part of the problem, Davies believed, was how an allegation of assault was received in the first place; and while he conceded investigations were changing for the better with Tidmarsh's 'whole story' approach, he thought many police officers still had a long way to go.

'Cops want to catch crooks, they don't want to be social workers,' he said. 'I'm not saying they don't care about the victims – it's just that a lot of police aren't equipped with the skills to deal with the complicated issues that sexual assaults offer up. A break-in rape – now that's a good job, a "feather in your cap" job.'

'Because there is an obvious villain?' I asked.

'Exactly. A crap job, however, is a fourteen-year-old goes to a party, says she was raped, the guys say she was with everyone. That's too hard.'

Davies spent twenty-nine years with the Victorian police force, the top cop at the sex crimes squad in his final years. It was here that he felt he could do his best work.

Intent on changing police and public perceptions of rape –

perceptions that in his mind often damaged victims because their experiences didn't suit the stereotypical scenario – Davies wrote letters to newspapers to clarify stories, met with journalists and tried to raise the profile of the squad so that the public understood its work. A fellow detective, Ken Ashworth, said Davies brought about a cultural change. 'When a prostitute would make a complaint, police used to say it was just a civil debt,' Davies told me later. 'They don't anymore.' But then, only two years into the job, Davies found himself suspended.

It was the rape allegations on the night of Collingwood's premiership win that partly triggered it. During a separate police integrity investigation, Davies was recorded confirming to journalists that Dayne Beams and John McCarthy were the footballers being questioned about the allegations. When the charge of unauthorised disclosure of information was laid against him, Davies was forced to resign.

Although he would never be a policeman again, Davies' desire to change police culture had not diminished. As he loaded me up with names of authors, papers and textbooks about police and media attitudes towards rape, I asked him about the process following an allegation of rape.

A neat explanation goes a little like this, explained Davies. If the complainant comes to the police immediately, hours or days after the incident, they undergo a medical examination. Then their statement is recorded and the 'what, where, when and who' are established. Once all or most of these boxes are ticked, police have a potential case to prosecute and the complainant will get their 'options' talk. 'This will involve talking them through the prosecution and court process.'

The process of the investigation, however, is rarely neat. The complainant's statement is invariably picked over for inconsistencies and credibility. 'They know that any weakness in credibility of the complainant will be seized on by the defence.' Davies added that this can often be done with a fair degree of scepticism. 'There's the, "C'mon, tell us what really happened" or "If I ring your boyfriend, what will he say? Do you have a boyfriend?"'

The complainant's initial reaction to the alleged assault is almost always interrogated, the general belief being that there are only two options available to a victim: fight or flight.

'But there's a third reaction,' he said, 'and it's the most common one. It's "freeze."' Like a rabbit caught in headlights, the vulnerable person simply seizes up, unable to flee or to fight. 'But that doesn't suit police, the media or the courts – you'll always have a defendant's lawyer saying, "Why didn't you scream?"'

Then there is the tricky scenario in which the complainant actually knows the offender. 'You'll have police asking, "If you were raped by this guy, then why did you go back and see him?"' But again, Davies said, the complainant's reactions are far from practised in such a situation, and in some instances they're second-guessing themselves. 'Especially when the guy they think may have raped them comes back to them the next day and says they "had a great night." She'll be like, "What? It was hell. Is this the same night we're talking about?" Often men will "retell" the situation and dress it up as something it wasn't.'

The options talk is a necessity, no matter how cold and pragmatic it may seem to the complainant. Carolyn Worth at the South Eastern Centre Against Sexual Assault told me about a situation in which a woman, after being told what she could expect during a trial, decided she would not be able to handle the cross-examination. The woman had Tourette's syndrome, explained Worth, sighing. 'She knew she wouldn't be able to withstand the questioning. The thing is, what made her not testify is likely to be the same reason her neighbour raped her. She was vulnerable, a perfect target.'

A friend of mine who was raped at a wedding reception when she was in her late teens was told quite pragmatically by a police officer and a sexual assualt counsellor that she would have to accept that she'd no doubt be ruining the wedding couple's memories of their special day if she decided to take the offender to trial.

'I was told that most of the wedding party would have to testify,' she said, adding that the options talk had been so discouraging that she had even started to question if the assault had happened, despite the physical evidence. 'I should have been encouraged to go through with it. I had a toxicology result proving that I had Rohypnol in my system from that night. Who knows how many others the same guy has done it to since?'

The options talk is also about police explaining what the complainant's chances are of getting a conviction – and if the prospects are low, then police will most likely be advising against pursuing the case, or will already have made the decision to suspend their investigations.

Davies believed police needed to be less focused on getting a win in court. 'The law is very specific about what is rape and what is not, but it's not being applied. We're not brave enough in our own prosecuting,' he said. 'I've heard numerous sergeants say, "Oh, it will never get up" and "The Office of Public Prosecutions, they just want a win." But we need to not focus so much on conviction, but keep putting these cases in front of juries and maybe one day they'll be more sophisticated in their understanding of rape.'

I wondered if this was why Justin was charged and the others who came under investigation on the same evening were not (Sarah's statement revealed she'd made multiple complaints against multiple protagonists) – because police assumed a jury would not be sophisticated enough to understand the nuances of the bedroom allegations, while the charges against Justin involved a classic rape stereotype. The setting was, after all, a dark alleyway.

'I had a sergeant come up to me recently,' Davies continued, 'and he's a good policeman, but even he said to me he was confused about what to do in a rape case he was investigating, that it just came down to "he said, she said." And I said, "How can you be confused? You charge him. Why not? You do the same with a robbery. If a complainant was robbed in the street and identified the assailant, the police would not hesitate in charging the offender."'

I was uneasy. 'But a rape charge is different, surely? I mean, you can't rub that off. It's a permanent stain.'

I wanted to agree entirely with Davies, to share completely in his horror at the treatment of rape complainants, but something kept snagging in my thoughts and it was Justin. His quiet and gentle manner threw me. When I looked at him in the dock, snared in a stereotypical rape scenario from the alleyway to the aftermath, he didn't seem to fit the stereotype that went with the story. A stereotype that seems to rely on a typology popularised in 1979 by Dr Nicholas Groth in his book *Men Who Rape*: the 'sadistic,' 'anger' or 'power' rapist, men varying in their motives but all premeditated in their hunt for vulnerable prey. Justin seemed like a boy in comparison.

But this was naïve. 'There is no type,' Dr Angela Williams, a forensic physician with much experience of rape cases, later said to me. 'I meet a lot of offenders, and not one is a guy hiding behind a tree. You can't pick them in a crowd, but they can pick out their victim – it is someone in a vulnerable position, be it a family member, an ex-partner or someone who is very drunk.'

Williams said in spite of commonly held beliefs about rape and rapists, only about one in a hundred offenders was the 'tree' man, the rape occurring in the alley, by the train tracks or in the bushes. Among her colleagues, these stereotypical scenarios were often referred to as 'rape myths.' 'You never hear about the husband who rapes his wife and brings her flowers the next day. Or the guy who's a top bloke, plays cricket at the local club and so on. And as a result, the victim looks at these myths and thinks no one is ever going to believe them.'

The same thing applied to the victims of rape: 'I meet all sorts of girls and women, they can be covered head to toe, in work attire, dressed for a nightclub, in gym gear, there is no pattern.'

And then there was the question of how to define rape itself.

\*

Was it 'rape-rape,' 'rapish' or just 'rapesque'? That was the question the American comedian Kristen Schaal asked on *The Daily Show with Jon Stewart* in 2011 in mock support of a proposed change to abortion legislation. Under the Republican bill, all funding for abortion stemming from rape would be cut unless it was a result of 'forcible' rape.

'You'd be surprised how many drugged, underage or mentally handicapped women have been gaming the system,' said Schaal tongue-in-cheek, wagging her finger. 'Sorry, ladies, the free abortion ride is over.' Acting bewildered, Jon Stewart asked, but isn't *all* rape forcible? Wide-eyed, Schaal shook her head. 'I'm not comfortable with that word, "all" rape. In truth,' she explained, 'there is a whole rainbow of rape, covering a wide spectrum of grey areas ... There's rape, and there's rape-rape.'

In recent years there has been ample opportunity for left-wing commentators to take the piss out of so-called rape apologists. Schaal was alluding to Whoopi Goldberg's confused stance towards the film director Roman Polanski, who by his own admission had given a thirteen-year-old girl drugs and champagne before having sex with her, after her mother had let him borrow her for the day for a *Vogue* magazine shoot in 1977.

In a televised chat following a recent attempt to extradite Polanski to the United States, Goldberg passionately defended him. 'I know it wasn't rape-rape. It was something else, but I don't believe it was rape-rape.'

In Britain, the controversial politician and writer George Galloway came under fire when he said that sexual assault allegations against Julian Assange amounted to no more than bad 'sexual etiquette.' 'Even taken at its worst, if the allegations made by these two women were true, 100 per cent true, and even if a camera in the room captured them, they don't constitute rape,' he said. 'At least not rape as anyone with any sense can possibly recognise it. And somebody has to say this. Woman A met Julian

Assange, invited him back to her flat, gave him dinner, went to bed with him, had consensual sex with him, claims that she woke up to him having sex with her again. This is something which can happen, you know. I mean, not everybody needs to be asked prior to each insertion.'

When Galloway refused to apologise for his remarks, he was fired as columnist on a Scottish political magazine. Several British barristers took the time to point out that Galloway's views were not reflected in English law. 'Waking up being penetrated is not an embarrassing event to be put down to experience but a frightening example of "sleep rape,"' wrote the barrister Felicity Gerry.

But the reality is – despite all of the commentary opining that rape is not a difficult concept to get one's head around, that it boils down to a simple 'no means no' and all discussion outside of that single-minded certainty is for rape apologists – rape is not always easy to establish or identify, let alone to confirm beyond reasonable doubt.

Proof of this is in the statistics. Fewer than 12 per cent of sexual assaults reported to police in Australia result in convictions. And this is through little fault of modern law, where reforms have continually tried to make up for centuries of ill treatment of rape complainants, and where the need for explicit consent is now clearly defined.

In part the confusion rests with us. And it's not necessarily because we're all misogynists. Unlike with most crimes, to apply the label of rape in some instances can be subjective. 'I know it was rape,' a friend once confided in me after a male acquaintance had helped her walk home, only to take advantage of her extreme drunkenness. 'At least, it was in the legal sense,' she said. 'But I don't want to call it rape.' It was not an act of denial, she believed – after all, she had taken great pains the next day to find out what exactly had occurred between them. But she just couldn't close the gap between her idea of rape and what had happened to her.

In most parts of Australia, a rape conviction is not based solely on the victim's lack of consent. In New South Wales, Victoria, South Australia, the Northern Territory and the ACT, proving this is only half of the job. To obtain a conviction, the prosecution must also prove the accused was *aware* that the victim was not or might not be consenting, or was indifferent to whether there was consent. Rape is as much a state of mind as it is an act.

Interestingly, Victoria – once considered the most progressive state in Australia for its sexual assault laws – is now said to have fallen foul of its own forward-thinking legislation. By claiming an honest belief in consent, no matter how outlandish, defendants have a new ace up their sleeves. 'Clever defence lawyers are using it to get their clients off,' Carolyn Worth told me. 'That way, even if the jury finds she wasn't consenting, he still believed she was, and he can avoid conviction.'

As a result, added Worth, numerous rape convictions have been overturned or appealed since 2007. In one case, the Victorian Court of Appeal ruled in favour of a man accused of raping an unconscious woman: he told the court he believed she had consented because she groaned as he undressed her. Another convicted man won a retrial because the judge presiding over his trial had not directed the jury to consider his state of mind. Court transcripts revealed the woman he'd been accused of raping had been so drunk she could barely walk out of a nightclub and had vomited twice – first in a pub and second in the backseat of a car where the defendant claimed to be having consensual sex with her. She then fell out of the car, injuring her chin and knee.

According to this law, a person who acts with a clear conscience is not culpable. But is this true – that to be guilty, you need to have an idea of doing something wrong? This was what a jury would have to decide about Justin. The prosecution claimed Sarah did not consent to having sex with Justin in the alley – but was he *aware* of this? Did he consider the possibility of her not consenting?

Justin told me that in the six weeks before he was charged, the police had secretly bugged his phone and accessed his text messages. The evidence they gathered, he believed, should have helped his case. He had made comments while unaware of being recorded that indicated a belief that his and Sarah's encounter had been consensual. 'But,' he said warily, 'there was a sting attached.' It was also revealed that he and his football mates had a 'rooting competition' going on.

I shrugged when Justin told me this, thinking of a piece of paper I'd kept when I was a teenager listing all the people I'd kissed, a question mark standing in for the names of those I had been too drunk to remember. It wasn't a rooting competition, but it was definitely a tally of sorts. Later, when I came across the so-called Spur Posse in America, a group of Californian high school boys who were investigated by police and had used a point system to compete sexually with one another – one point for penetration and only one point allowed for each girl – I realised the possible implications of the rooting competition. With such an explicit intention to get laid, how can such a competition *not* go too far? How much premeditation to get laid was too much?

When I was thirteen, a boy a couple of years older than me plied me with tequila, which I happily consumed. I later learned it was his plan – a plan others at the party were well aware of – to get me drunk so he could fuck me. Unfortunately for him, I passed out while it was still daylight and was carried home by a chorus of friends. But had he succeeded, would the fifteen-year-old have been a rapist? If I were incapable of consenting, yes, that would fulfil the performative element of rape, but what about his state of mind? The premise of the 2007 teen flick *Superbad* has the main character trying to organise a loot of alcohol to impress a girl and get her drunk so he can have sex with her. Of course, it all works out in the end: it turns out the girl doesn't drink (what a good girl, and a handy plot-swerve around the messy idea of consent) and the two get to know each other in a decent way, but was there any mention of the main character – a nice gentle boy – being a rapist in the making? Of course not.

Can there be such a thing as an ignorant rapist, a thoughtless rapist, an opportunistic rapist or even a rapist by mistake? And does a jury's failure to convict such a man, as Glenn Davies believed, show a lack of sophistication and understanding about rape? Or is there a deep sense of unease among the public about labelling certain young men rapists? Put him in a basket, sure, but not in the same one as the hiding-in-the-bushes predator, the drink-spiker or the husband who treats his wife as his property and assaults her as he wishes.

\*

As I turned to face the doors in the elevator, a woman in spectacles and a dress quickly put her hand in between them and held them open. She shepherded a group into the lift. Ten to fifteen people bustled inside with me. The woman stood at the door with more people waiting behind her. 'Level 7,' she said to the people in the lift, 'Level 7.' And then, as she let the doors close, she said one last time, 'Level 7.' As soon as she was gone from view, the people inside the lift laughed. 'I feel like we're back at school,' one said.

Then as the elevator rose, one joked, 'I can't remember, was it Level 4?'

'Nah, Level 5,' another quipped.

But then, when the lift opened at Level 6, a couple of them wandered out absentmindedly. Potential jurors.

It was day three of Justin's trial and the courtroom was full of ordinary people called in for jury duty. Of the fifty-odd assembled, twelve would be selected. 'Trial by jury,' said Judge Taft, 'is an essential plank of our system of justice.' He addressed the group, explaining that individuals would be called out randomly and were to make their way to the back of the room. There, they would either get the nod to walk to the front of the room and take a seat in the jury box, or be 'challenged' by lawyers for the defence or 'stood aside' by the prosecution – in which case they would return to their seats.

Both defence and prosecution were not required to give any reason for their misgivings and were allowed six challenges each.

The judge's associate called out the name and occupation of each panel member. A former WorkSafe employee and a Sri Lankan accountant, both male, made their way unimpeded to the jury box. Then an unemployed female childcare worker was introduced. Justin Dyer's solicitor was standing next to Justin just outside the dock and gave him a nudge. 'Challenge,' Justin called out. The woman stopped, swivelled and returned to her seat. A young female administrative worker was called up. 'Challenge,' said Justin again. And so on, until he had used up all his challenges. A young female nurse and a beauty therapist then managed to sneak through, but the final jury was this: ten men, mostly middle-aged, and two women.

From the moment they took their seats, the jurors had been the centre of attention, the lawyers and judge alert to their needs. But as they filed out at the end of the day and the door was shut behind them, I noticed the charade drop a little. As I watched the barristers and judge return to their legal triangle of barely decipherable, coded language, I realised that the jury members were more like precious children than wise sages. It was as if they would be kept in a large dark room with the occasional torch shedding light on a piece of evidence or a witness, but the rest of the time were to grope their way around or, at precarious times, let themselves be led carefully around great potholes of backstory.

# CHAPTER 8

'Whatever the barrister says is not evidence,' said Crown prosecutor Ryan in his opening address to the jury, warning them to take what he *and* defence counsel Thomas said with a degree of wariness. The prosecutor was a somewhat bumbling, ruddy-cheeked, red-haired lawyer with watery eyes and a fondness for homely adages such as 'What's good for the goose is good for the gander.'

Ryan then told the story of three friends – Sarah, Olivia and Tom – and how they began their Saturday night with drinks at their residential college before heading to Eve nightclub in South Melbourne, where Sarah had organised to meet Nate Cooper, a boy she had first met two weeks earlier. Around 4.40 a.m., Sarah and Nate left Eve and headed back to Nate's house on Dorcas Street. By the time they arrived, Ryan stated ominously, 'There was a number of men at the house already, including two Collingwood football players.' While Sarah was there, she was in the bedroom, and was unaware that some people had left and others had arrived, including Justin Dyer.

Within an hour, said Ryan – skipping over what had happened in the house – Sarah left and became aware of Justin only when she was on the street. He asked her where she was going; she said she was going home. At the entrance to an alley, he said, 'Come down here with me first,' and began to kiss her. Startled, she pulled her face away and he put his fingers up her dress, moved her undies aside and 'digitally penetrated' her. This was the 'first count.'

Sarah pushed him and said, 'No, stop it, I want to go home,' and tried to run. Justin stopped her. She tried to get away from him on two or three occasions. He pushed up her skirt, bent her over and penetrated her from behind. During this time, he called her Sarah. 'She was perplexed,' Ryan said. 'She doesn't remember meeting him.'

'I don't want to do this,' she said, to which he replied, 'Nah, just let it finish.'

Sarah, after running out of the alley, continued towards Clarendon Street. Justin caught up with her. They had a conversation and even swapped numbers, Sarah agreeing to this because she was scared. They got in a cab and first went to Elwood, where Justin lived. In the cab, Justin kept insisting on making a date to see her the next day; she refused at first, but finally relented. Then, after the cab stopped outside the block of flats where he lived, dropping him off, the driver took her home.

Sarah had been trying to get in touch with her friend Tom and finally did so when she was in her room at the college. He went to her room. During this time, Justin called and texted. The first message read, 'How are you feeling this morning?' Ryan concluded to the jury that he had done this to keep his control over her.

Then Ryan switched and retold the story, this time from Justin's police statement. The accused man told police he was at a function to celebrate the premiership, where he had eight beers and a few shots, and then he went to Eve nightclub, where he consumed around ten drinks. He left Eve at 5 a.m. and went to the house on Dorcas Street, where he said he saw the complainant.

He spoke with her and offered to go with her to get a cab, took her by the hand, and they kissed on the street. He needed to piss and went up a laneway to do so. Afterwards he called her up to him and they kissed and fondled each other. She gave him head and he asked to have sex.

Ryan paused now for emphasis. 'He says, "She pushed her dress up and bent over" and then *of her own volition –*' Ryan said the words singly and mockingly – 'she stopped and went down on him.'

Then she stood up. 'I've got to go to this party.'

'Can you finish me off?' Justin said.

'Yes' – and she went down on him again, then she said, 'No, I've got to go.'

*

*Can you finish me off?*

When we heard that line, I and the young female ABC journalist sitting beside me flinched.

During a break, I found her outside the court, watching as the photographers and TV cameramen rallied to get a picture of Justin as he emerged from the building. She pointed him out to her photographer and then stood back. We started chatting and I asked her what she thought about Justin's account, in particular the *Can you finish me off?* line.

'Well, you know …' she said, before trailing off.

'Heard it a million times before?'

She laughed. 'Not a million times! But yes, definitely heard that one before.'

I nodded. 'Me too.'

The Crown prosecutor had scoffed at the ridiculousness of Justin's version of the evening – but it hadn't sounded that ridiculous at all. In fact, I thought with a shudder, it sounded all too familiar.

*

Malcolm Thomas was a straight-talker. Young-looking, with a serious face and prematurely grey hair, perhaps as a result of all that solemnity, he exuded none of the blokey comradely jousting of which David Galbally was fond, the kind of 'We're mates, aren't we?' performance that makes my skin prickle. As I watched Thomas interact with Judge Taft, a man with a no-nonsense air, I thought that Justin was better off without Galbally. The QC's obvious ties to the inner world of football might have been disastrous for his case.

In his opening, Thomas bullet-pointed the evening for the jury. Justin Dyer and Sarah Wesley walked down the stairs together and into the street. Went into the lane and had sex. They left the lane. There was an exchange of phone numbers. Then, observed by witnesses, they got into a taxi together and had a discussion about where they were heading, before deciding to go to Elwood first and making an arrangement to meet up the next day. Justin later sent a text message to follow up.

'What's in dispute?' Thomas asked rhetorically. 'That the sex was consensual,' he answered. 'Justin did not believe it was not.'

It did not take Thomas long to get to the crux of his defence. 'Is Sarah Wesley a liar?' he asked the jury. 'We say she is a liar.'

Thomas referred to the Crown's version of events – that Sarah had first become aware of Justin on the street, that he was a stranger – but continued, 'We have witnesses who saw them in the house and on the street.'

'Were they affectionate, kissing?' he asked again. 'Are there witnesses who observed that happening? Yes.'

'Can she not remember, or is it because she is a liar?'

Thomas went on to examine Justin's behaviour. His style was clipped, pragmatic and simple – there was no lawyerly jargon or attempts to make a profound impact on the jury. Instead he laid out the 'facts' without fanfare, implying that, surely, they spoke for themselves.

'Why has Dyer given a woman he has supposedly raped his phone number, taken her to his home and called her the next day? Because he wants to catch up with her. Consistent with what happens after consensual sex.'

Thomas continued in this manner, asking and answering rhetorical questions, until he came to what he described as 'real' evidence.

In spite of having more than a few witnesses to corroborate Justin's side of the story, Thomas emphasised that he wouldn't be relying on these. Instead he waved a wad of papers in the air. They were, he explained, documents relating to the use of mobile phones throughout the evening.

'Phone records are central to this case,' he said, and to remind the jury of his central contention that Sarah Wesley was a liar, added, 'People lie, phone records don't lie.'

*

I felt a flash of anger each time Thomas said 'liar.' It rose up in me and I took it out on my notepad, pressing my pencil hard against the paper. Later, when I looked over my notes, I realised just how inarticulate I had been in expressing why this made me angry. Thick and bold scribbling and crosshatching spilled illegibly across the page.

Was it an old-school feminist bile rising up in me – rage that Thomas was playing the age-old card of the lying female? Women have been cast as deceitful characters since before it was written that Eve ate the apple. The New Zealand criminologist Jan Jordan, in her paper 'Beyond Belief: Police, Rape and Women's Credibility,' referred to a 'Witchhunters Guidebook' published in 1484 that describes women as defective from the very start, formed as they were from a bent rib. 'Imperfect, and inherently deceptive,' wrote Jordan. 'These ideas filtered through society, evident in legal, medical and criminological thought.'

Police investigating rape, Jordan pointed out, were hampered by such perceptions. She quoted Detective Inspector Alan Firth, who wrote in 1975 that 'Women and children complainants in sexual matters are notorious for embroidery or complete fabrication of complaints.' Firth continued:

It should be borne in mind that except in the case of a very young child, the offence of rape is extremely unlikely to have been committed against a woman who does not immediately show signs of extreme violence.

If a woman walks into a police station and complains of rape with no signs of such violence, she must be closely interrogated. Allow her to make her statement to a Policewoman and then drive a horse and cart through it. It is always advisable if there is any doubt of the truthfulness of her allegations to call her an outright liar.

That this kind of thinking has been the status quo for centuries (unless of course it was a white woman accusing a black man of rape, and then perceptions were reversed) and only recently addressed is enough to make any accusation that a rape complainant is a 'liar' seem a harking back to the bad old days.

But at the same time, the opposing position also sat uneasily with me. In 2000, the Russian-American journalist and writer Cathy Young wrote in *Salon* that in the past thirty years:

> rape victims' advocacy has gone from challenging clearly unjust practices (such as jury instructions that 'unchaste character' could be held against the woman's credibility) to insisting that if a woman feels raped, the man must be guilty. As legal scholar Catharine MacKinnon put it, 'Feminism is built on believing women's accounts of sexual use and abuse by men.'

Particularly in the United States it seems that these two opposing biases are more prominent than ever: the notion that all women always tell the truth when it comes to allegations of rape is increasingly common, despite it being as ridiculous as the notion that women are mostly liars when they say they have been raped.

Wendy Murphy, a former sex crimes prosecutor and law professor, is a regular US commentator on CNN, Fox News and other channels whenever an issue of sexual assault arises. On one occasion, in response to the suggestion that surely everyone must be presumed innocent before being proven guilty, she said angrily, 'I'm really tired of people suggesting that you're some- how un-American if you don't respect the presumption of inno- cence, because you know what that sounds like to a victim? Presumption you're a liar.'

It's one or the other, it seems. She's a liar, or he's a rapist.

Gazing at my angry pencil marks, I realised that my frustra- tion had little to do with being made out of a bent rib or other- wise. It was possible that Sarah had lied about aspects of the night's events. I could even understand the strategy behind Thomas's method. A jury must be convinced 'beyond reasonable doubt' in order to convict, and so all the defence needs to do is introduce an element of doubt about the accusation or the accuser. This tends to result in a situation in which it seems as though the complainant is on trial. If Sarah had misled the police or jury in any way, how could the jury possibly *not* doubt her entire story?

But does one lie invalidate an entire experience, and if not, then how many lies does it take to negate an allegation of rape?

'Sometimes a victim will change their story to suit a rape myth and unfortunately there is usually a story to be told, but not the one we're hearing,' Dr Angela Williams told me.

Glenn Davies agreed. 'If she alters her story to fit a rape myth, then she's out. She's lied. There is no attempt to peel back the dramatic storytelling to the ordinary crime, to find out what actually happened.'

The tag 'liar' is so absolute – the schoolyard definition has it that a lie is always malicious, that there is no truth in the vicinity of a lie. Yet a victim, as Williams and Davies suggested, may alter her story to bring it into accord with the accepted idea of rape – especially if she doesn't understand that the term can be applied to scenarios where there is no physical violence, where she didn't physically resist or scream for help. A lie is here used to stand in for something that one has no language for, for which there is no accepted remedy.

*

Dr Lauren Rosewarne, a social and political sciences lecturer at the University of Melbourne, had written on ABC's *The Drum*, 'A woman can't be a little bit pregnant, she can't be a little bit dead, she can't be a little bit equal, and she most certainly can't be a little bit sexually assaulted. If consent is absent, rape has occurred. There is no grey.' But when I asked her if it was possible for someone to feel raped even if they weren't raped, she squirmed. 'Oh, you're opening a can of worms there.'

She thought for a moment and then said slowly, 'Yes. I think it's possible. Many feminists see this as extremely dangerous to bring up because prosecuting rape is so hard. It reminds me of what people said when documenting the Jewish Holocaust – "Don't exaggerate," they warned, because it would devalue the rest.

'Most women have had sex and not really wanted to. And it highlights the fact that women still have trouble articulating their needs and wants. And that places a high burden on men to be able to read the signs. Women smile way more than men when they're uncomfortable.'

I nodded, well aware of my own tendency to smile when feeling unsure of myself. We're polite, too, I thought, especially in situations when we have more than enough reason to be rude. I recalled from *The First Stone* Helen Garner's memory of sitting in an empty train compartment when a stranger entered, sat close to her and eventually asked her to 'give him a kiss.'

'I *let* him kiss me on the lips,' wrote Garner, 'out of embarrassment, or politeness, or passivity, or lack of a clear sense of what *I* wanted, which was for him to dematerialise at once.'

The time it took for Garner to react seemed glacial. It took a passerby on the station platform glancing in at them for her to snap into action, see the absurdity of her situation and disentangle herself from his advances – advances, she wrote, which were neither violent, forceful or threatening; there was only a 'steady, almost imperceptible persistence.'

Is this the grey zone I'm trying to put my finger on, that glacial space between a man's action and a woman's reaction? And in that slow underwater place, is it a race? To see how far, how much he can get before she surfaces? Or is he also underwater? Must he become an interpreter of smiles? How many women and men are caught out in this grey zone?

Once a person is in the police station reporting a rape complaint, there is a presumption the complainant is either lying or telling the truth. But, as the criminologist Jan Jordan pointed out:

The confusion and ambiguity surrounding sexual negotiation and forceful seduction may mean that, in some situations, the complainant feels as if she has been victimised and is genuinely unsure as to whether she was raped.

And what if, as often as women encounter disbelief and suspicion, there is also the possibility that police and even peers apply pressure, perhaps subconsciously, so that a person seeks to make their story conform, not only to accepted ideas of how rape occurs and how one reacts to it, but also to the category of rape full stop?

Once under the questioning gaze of outsiders, is there room for a person to explore a disturbing sexual encounter without concluding that it was either rape or that they were to blame?

In an essay in *Playboy* in 1973, Germaine Greer coined the term 'petty rape,' saying that:

> Morally, those of us who have a high opinion of sex cannot accept the idea of passive consent … we must insist that evidence of positive desire alone dignifies sexual intercourse and makes it joyful. From a proud and passionate woman's point of view, anything less is rape.

But anything less is not rape. And how does an ordinary person, a young female not yet a proud and passionate woman, articulate that? That they got fucked, treated like shit and yet for some reason they lay back and 'took it'?

\*

After the lawyers' opening speeches, the jurors were bundled into a mini-van and taken to South Melbourne, an old suburb that had begun as a slum and since transformed into a fashionable hub of cafés, antique shops, fancy baby strollers, renovated terraces and picture-perfect parks. As if on a school excursion – some of them taking notes on pads provided – the jurors were led down Dorcas Street, starting at 303, a three-storey townhouse in a row of identical modern houses made of orange and grey concrete slabs. Next they milled around the alleyways – the bluestone lane that Kathy Hackett's bedroom window looked onto and the laneway that Justin had identified. The jurors peered at Hackett's rented house, a dark, squat redbrick worker's cottage, and wandered down the laneway mottled with graffiti.

Earlier, Judge Taft had warned the jurors that they were not investigators; the visit to South Melbourne was simply to help them get their bearings, but I imagined them looking for clues regardless, staring at the bricks, the dusty glass windows and the fat palm tree looming out of someone's backyard, willing them to break their silence. Further down Dorcas Street, just before it opened onto Clarendon Street, a busy shopping strip, was Emerald Hill Place, the laneway backing onto the shops, a corridor of brick walls and roller doors, where Justin said he and Sarah had sex. Then, finally, the jurors stood on Clarendon Street, noting where others saw Sarah and Justin that night after the alleyway incident, waiting together for a cab.

And so the trial began. And then it ran off its tracks. That evening, the *Herald Sun* website published a photograph of Justin under the headline, 'Rapist free to go nightclubbing after court alters curfew.' The article that followed read, 'A brute who raped a 14-year-old has persuaded a court to change his curfew, which will free him to go nightclubbing.' The line beneath the photo of Justin read simply, 'Beware of this beast.' The News Limited newspaper, Australia's largest, had got its convicted rapists and persons facing rape charges mixed up. A stunning mistake. But had a juror seen it? Had a person that knew a juror seen it? And the witnesses, had they seen it?

# CHAPTER 9

'How the Dickens did this happen?' snapped Judge Taft. The jury had been cooped up in the back room for an hour now, after being told a legal matter had come up.

Prosecutor Ryan, his wig askew, half-stood and gestured. 'The man in the grey pin-striped suit behind me will tell you, Your Honour, and is it better that you hear from him first to be informed?'

Taft glowered, looking at the man hovering behind Ryan. 'Yes, it may be. A familiar face.'

Mr Quill, a man in his thirties or early forties with blond hair and wearing a fashionable suit, bowed a little as he stood at the lectern.

'Your Honour,' he began, offering an 'unreserved and absolute apology' on behalf of the Herald & Weekly Times.

He went on. 'I can also inform Your Honour that my client gets articles legalled on a daily basis, an hourly basis, but ultimately human error – the best systems in the world cannot overcome human error and that is what has occurred on this occasion … I can tell Your Honour that my client will be taking action about this and taking it very, very seriously.'

'This court may too, Mr Quill,' growled Taft.

Quill jumped a little. 'Indeed, Your Honour, I would urge Your Honour and my client would urge Your Honour not to do so in the circumstances, it being a human error –'

Taft cut him off. 'Let us confine your involvement now to establishing the facts.'

\*

Justin's phone, his mother's phone and his brothers' phones had all started ringing at the same time as friends told them to log on to the *Herald Sun*'s website. Justin felt sick. Carol started to cry. The article was one of the first items on the website and no doubt not far off from becoming a 'most popular story.'

The family called their lawyer. Justin's older brother, who had just flown to Melbourne to be with them, started taking screen shots of the site. No one knew how long it had been up for. Then, not long afterwards, the story vanished. Someone in the *Herald Sun* office had cottoned on. But the link and photo still appeared on Google.

Next morning, Malcolm Thomas stood up to inform the judge that the day would not be able to proceed as normal.

Judge Taft's face darkened. 'This is the problem with new media,' he said.

Thomas announced that the defence would be applying for a discharge of the jury and adjournment of the trial. Taft was reluctant.

'Why can't the jury be told an egregious error has occurred?'

he asked Thomas, who shook his head.

'That's not sufficient.'

Taft then outlined the issues that needed to be considered. 'Has prejudice arisen and how is it overcome? Can it be overcome immediately?' This is in the interests of the complainant as well as the accused, he said firmly. 'Justice delayed is justice denied.'

As the judge got up, we all stood. Disappearing into a room behind the court, he pulled the door hard behind him, black gown swishing furiously. If it wasn't one of those heavy, slow-shutting 'unable to vent one's frustration' doors, I'm sure it would have slammed.

\*

Later, when Taft returned to the court, Thomas stood up to announce that the Google link and image had 'elevated, rather than receded.' Quill tried to reassure the court, saying that while his client didn't yet have exact numbers, he had been told that the maximum time the story and image were online was twenty minutes, while views were in the 'single digits.'

'What about the Google link?' asked Taft.

Quill looked back at his assistant, who darted out of the room.

The day avalanched onwards. There was adrenaline running through the Dyer camp – well, through everyone but Justin, who sat quietly in the foyer during the breaks watching as his family upped the ante on the drama, speaking to friends on their phones and bringing up the screen shot of the newspaper's mix-up to show one another. I asked Justin if he wanted the trial to be adjourned – another delay would mean almost two years of his life spent waiting to hear his fate. 'They,' he said, gesturing at his lawyers, 'they think it's a good thing.' He rubbed his face, his red-rimmed eyes. 'I don't know.'

*

It was the 3AW talkshow host Neil Mitchell who had first broadcast the names of the two Collingwood players, Dayne Beams and John McCarthy. He said he identified the pair in the name of fairness, consistency and because 'secrecy benefited no one': not to clarify the rumours was unfair to other Collingwood players and in similar situations other football players had been named. 'So why should Collingwood players be any different here?'

Football insiders, on the other hand, raged. On his Triple M radio show, the Collingwood president, Eddie McGuire, called Mitchell 'irresponsible' and a 'self-appointed, self-important windbag,' while the club put out a statement saying it is 'grossly unfair to name anyone – and [we] will not do so – as the investigation is still in its early days.'

The AFL and the Players Association also hit out. An AFL statement said that all parties involved were treating the investigation with the utmost importance: 'But anyone involved in a serious matter like this – whether they play AFL or come from any other walk of life – is entitled to a presumption of innocence and is entitled to not be pre-judged or paraded publicly.'

After Mitchell named the pair, other media outlets followed suit. The *Herald Sun*, whose editor had earlier cited a 'moral issue,' suddenly felt freed from such inhibitions and published the Collingwood duo's names and photographs on the front page.

Mitchell claimed that Collingwood had threatened legal action, and said it was wrong that he could be sued. 'I believe I can name them as long as I make clear the solid possibility that they've done nothing wrong, even if a sexual assault occurred, and we don't even know that. They may just be witnesses, not participants.'

'He talks of fairness?' McGuire responded. 'This is the hypocrisy of Neil Mitchell.' Mitchell promoted the right of all people to be equal in the eyes of the law, 'unless they're someone he wants to name.'

*

In 1977, a Columbia University law professor, Vivian Berger, cautioned against 'sacrificing the legitimate rights of the accused person on the altar of Women's Liberation.' Recent decades have seen Western countries introduce much-needed 'rape shield' laws. In most instances, this means the complainant's identity is protected, stemming from the idea that shame is part of a rapist's power over their victim, a wound that lingers long after the act, and that publishing a complainant's name would only further that violation.

Another major protective measure for complainants is the prohibition on their sexual history being brought up in court. In some areas, although this is rare, the name of the defendant is also suppressed until charges have been laid. Queensland, South Australia and the Northern Territory all offer anonymity during committal hearings, but the defendant can be named if the case proceeds to trial. In Victoria and New South Wales, the homes of the AFL and NRL, there are no restrictions on naming the accused.

'It's a permanent stain,' I'd said to Glenn Davies when he argued police ought to lay charges for rape just as they would for any other crime. 'You can't rub it off.' Ironically, I'd used language more associated with a rape victim than a person accused of rape. Stigma and shame are hallmarks of rape, both during and in the aftermath.

'I felt like everyone was looking at me and talking about me,' Justin said of his increasing fear of going out. Good, some people may say. Serves him right. And often, in the minds of many working in the area of sexual assault – counsellors, prosecutors and police – trial by media may be the only 'true' justice available to victims of rape. In the *Age*, Marg D'Arcy, from Melbourne's Centre Against Sexual Assault, had told the sex therapist and clinical psychologist Bettina Arndt that defendants ought to be named because the chance of prosecution in sex crimes is so low that 'victims take solace from public naming of the accused.'

'A little bit of him is being held accountable,' said D'Arcy, adding that she was convinced most defendants deserved it. 'What we are dealing with in relation to sexual assault is far from innocent men being wrongly charged. The huge majority of men who commit sexual assault never, ever come anywhere near the courts.'

Others, such as Germaine Greer, are so disillusioned with the outcome of rape cases that they have suggested victims bypass the legal system altogether and use the media to 'name and shame' rapists online instead of reporting the crime to police. Speaking in Britain two years ago, where, at the time, the conviction rate of rapes recorded by police was 6 per cent, Greer said, 'I wish there were an online rapists register and that it was kept up to date, because we know the courts can't get it right.'

In July 2012, an American teenager, Savannah Dietrich, faced jail time for tweeting the names of her attackers, who had pleaded guilty to sexually assaulting her after she passed out at a party. Months later, she learned that graphic pictures of the assault and of her semi-undressed were taken and shared with others.

Dietrich took to her Twitter account during the trial in a Kentucky juvenile court after she learned the two boys had been offered, to her mind, a lenient plea deal – community service and undergoing a sex offender treatment course. Their criminal records would be immediately expunged once they turned twenty. In turn, Dietrich was informed of a gag order on speaking about the case.

'They said I can't talk about it or I'll be locked up,' one of her tweets read. 'So I'm waiting for them to read this and lock me up. Fuck justice.'

'If reporting a rape only got me to the point that I'm not allowed to talk about it, then I regret it,' she wrote on her Facebook wall. 'I regret reporting it.'

Her tweets produced a groundswell of support. The media swamped her and, unusually, were able to report her name after she told journalists that she wanted her case to be public, that she had no faith in the court system.

What, though, if the accused is innocent? Is it okay to sacrifice a few good men for the greater good? And if someone misuses the power of such an accusation, does a defendant have any protection against that?

Adding to the difficulty, similar but clashing considerations often produce a stalemate in rape cases. That some believe rape defendants ought to be hung out to dry in a public forum because conviction is highly unlikely is also why a defendant ought not to be named. The charges, the allegations, can't be rubbed out. As the public has become more educated about rape, it is widely understood that the low rate of rape convictions is less about whether a rape happened or not than whether it can be proven. So when a defendant walks free from a court, the cloud hanging over him walks out with him.

*

Quill's assistant returned to the courtroom: the numbers were in.

The article was up for twenty-three minutes between 10 and 11 p.m., Quill said, and although he was unable to get an exact number of homepage views, they had calculated an average. In that hour, the homepage was viewed 16,139 times, which worked out to over 6000 views in twenty-three minutes, while the link to the actual article was clicked on 1377 times. Google had acceded to the takedown request, but, Quill explained, some people might still have cached versions on their computers.

Two options now remained: to discharge the jury and adjourn the trial, or to provide the jury and witnesses with a clear account of the defendant's prior convictions – which in Justin's case were none, thus distancing him from the 'Beware of this Brute' article, while not contaminating anyone who hadn't seen or heard of it.

Judge Taft pondered the predicament. 'If not adjourned, can the risk be met?' He retreated to his chambers to consider.

\*

It had been a long day. In the foyer, people stood and stretched while they stared out of the windows at the grey city, the last light sliding across the car park below, their necks clicking. The Dyer family looked exhausted, a night of no sleep catching up with them.

I thought about them returning to their suitcases and their beds, and falling asleep in their suits.

\*

Judge Taft outlined the events of the day, describing the *Herald Sun* article as 'an egregious error.'

The defence, he continued, had applied for a discharge and adjournment based on the offending publication's influence. But what had been published was a falsehood, he countered, and therefore surely easier to rectify.

'The mischief that has occurred can be carefully and appropriately overcome,' said Judge Taft, as he delivered his ruling.

The trial, he said, would continue.

# CHAPTER 10

It was around 7 a.m. when Sarah got home. There she phoned Tom and he came to her room. By noon, her parents were also there and the police were on their way. Sarah went to the Royal Women's Hospital, and then the police drove her up and down the streets of South Melbourne, trying to find the townhouse and the alleyway. It wasn't until much later that Sunday, when it was dark, that the police put their notepads away and turned their recorder off and Sarah was allowed to close her eyes.

From the moment when Sarah spoke to police to the day when they pressed charges against Justin, she would have been watched, examined, her credibility tested. In a small qualitative study of New Zealand detectives, the criminologist Jan Jordan found the factors that come into play when police doubt a rape complaint range from drunkenness or being stoned, delayed reporting, if there had been previous consensual sex with the accused, a history of rape or rape allegations, abuse or psychiatric disturbance, perceived immorality or intellectual impairment.

'What is generally not questioned,' said Jordan, 'are the ways in which the very same cues the police see as indicating the complainant is a "slut" may be the very factors that make her vulnerable to rape.' Consider, for example, a person's sense of entitlement to a so-called slut – 'She's practically been through the entire team, why not me?'

Another factor is if the complainant sought to conceal from police aspects of the incident – for example, if she was high or had been flirting with the accused – in other words, if the complainant was trying to avoid being stereotyped. 'Victims of rape are caught in a double-bind situation,' said Jordan, 'whereby they know they will not be regarded as credible if they are perceived as "immoral," yet will be viewed as even less credible if they are detected trying to conceal their "immorality."'

Jordan outlined the case of Malcolm Rewa, who was eventually caught and tried for forty-five counts of rape involving twenty-seven women in New Zealand in the late 1990s. Most of Rewa's victims were well educated, professional and white, and many had been attacked in their own homes while sleeping. They were 'credible' victims and in this sense the attacker, a Maori man and a bikie, was the ideal rapist stereotype.

However, a couple of Rewa's victims weren't 'perfect'– most importantly, one of the first women who had made a complaint to police in 1987 was, unlike his later victims, able to name Rewa as her attacker.

She was one of his few Maori victims, as well as one of the only women to have her own previous criminal convictions, factors that were perceived by police as undermining her credibility. Their dismissal of her testimony left Rewa free to attack a further known 26 women before this woman's case was eventually heard in the 1998 trial, at which he was finally convicted of the crimes committed against her.

And yet, Jordan also noted, police are in a difficult position, having to tread a 'fine line between the victim and the accused as they attempt to preserve the balance of justice and guard against the possibilities of wrongful conviction.'

When I asked Glenn Davies how he thought a rape complainant ought to be interviewed, he replied, 'I think you respond in a believing manner and then corroborate,' adding that in his investigations he was after 'a result that truly reflected what happened. Not true or false, but what happened.'

And indeed, this is what moves a rape case forward – whether there are enough angles for it to be adequately tested. Yet there is an obvious problem with corroborating an allegation of rape. A rape is often like no other crime, especially murder. There is no body left at the scene. A sexual assault often involves a 'he said, she said' scenario, while the forensic aftermath of a rape can just as easily be passed off as the aftermath of consensual sex. 'There's this great disparity,' Davies said. 'You ask officers what they think is the second most serious crime next to murder and they'll inevitably say "rape" – and yet it is a crime with the lowest conviction rate.'

Back in the days of no DNA tests, rapists could simply deny any sexual relations had occurred, while today the worst thing a guilty defendant can say is, 'We didn't have sex.'

'We had sex, but it was consensual,' is the way to go – or in Victoria you could get away with saying, 'I *believed* it was consensual.'

Historically, the common law had it that a rape conviction could not occur without independent evidence – be it circumstantial or at least two witnesses to speak to a given fact. The law later gave way to allowing trials based solely on a complainant's word, but the judge was required to give a judicial warning, known as the 'corroboration warning,' to the jury about the dangers of convicting on the word of the complainant alone.

Advocates for reform battled these requirements, believing that such a warning too easily influenced juries not to convict, and that, as with all trials, due process was sufficient to detect any false accusation – in other words, the corroboration warning was discriminatory, particularly as the word of a complainant was considered sufficient for a conviction in cases of robbery or physical assault. Advocates also believed the corroboration warning originated in a misogynistic belief that women were untrustworthy and inclined to lie.

Others, however, argued the warning was necessary, that it sprang not from the nature of the witness but from the nature of the offence, as issues and motives surrounding allegations of rape are inherently more complicated than in other crimes.

In most parts of Australia, the United States and the United Kingdom, the requirement for a corroboration warning was abolished in the early eighties. Such a warning is now left to the discretion of the presiding judge. 'Thank goodness,' wrote the Manhattan sex-crimes prosecutor Linda Fairstein, that the victim's 'testimony – when it is credible – is all that is needed to convict a rapist, as it is any other criminal.'

But, as Cathy Young pointed out in *Salon*, there was another way to see such changes:

Of course, it then follows that to be 'fair,' we should convict defendants in rape cases on less evidence – and give the accuser's word more weight – than in other crimes. Which makes those old sexist warnings about how hard it is for an innocent man to defend himself against a charge of rape ring uncomfortably true.

Without corroboration, we are left only with credibility. Was Sarah Wesley credible? For the police and Director of Public Prosecutions to take her allegation this far, she must have been. But what is credible? In such cases, it is the ability to tell a story that is convincing and plausible. But is this not, to a degree and by necessity, a performance? And if so, how credible is a conviction that is based on performance alone?

\*

Sarah was the first to give evidence. The court was cleared. I stood and pushed through the heavy doors to the foyer. Except for Carol, who had permission to stay, Justin's family and girlfriend filed out behind me. The doors clicked as the tipstaff locked them. It was almost noon.

Yesterday there had been a palpable feeling of righteousness among the Dyers. Sure, Justin and his family had been more than upset by the *Herald Sun*'s screw-up, but it was a tangible screw-up – something they could set their sights on and fight. They weren't jousting at this ghost of a girl, a girl they couldn't see, an incident they couldn't take a screen shot of on their phones and say, 'See? See?' Yesterday it was as if the red had flooded back into their cheeks, but today the colour had leached out again.

Time moved like ice and we waited, looking at our phones. Intermittently one of us would walk over to the water bubbler – women putting their hands over the tops of their blouses to stop them from gaping open, men holding their ties flat against their shirts – and bend over to catch the cool metallic-tasting water, hands swiping at our mouths when we'd finished.

Inside the courtroom, the little diorama of activity continued. Sarah appeared by remote camera on a screen placed above the witness box. Justin was tucked away at the back of the room where she could not see him. The jury was led in. Then, in his methodical style, Ryan walked Sarah through the evening, asking about Eve nightclub, how she arrived at the townhouse and how she left it, the appearance of a 'stranger' on the street, and then the alley. Like quilters, the jury stitched her staccato answers into a story, a narrative. I imagined Justin's stony, unreadable face as Sarah answered the Crown's questions, describing each count of rape, and the jurors not just listening – but staring. Staring at Sarah and stealing glances at Justin, trying to surmise the truth from each flick of the eyes, squeeze it from each twist of the hands.

When the court doors were unlocked again, I was told that the defence's cross-examination of Sarah would take the rest of the day and resume after the weekend. I dropped out of the wait. I put my notepad in my bag, said goodbye to the Dyers and walked past the security guards and their X-ray machines, out of the County Court.

# CHAPTER II

'Mr Smith, you were held up at gunpoint on the corner of First and Main?'

'Yes.'

'Did you struggle with the robber?'

'No.'

'Why not?'

'He was armed.'

'Then you made a conscious decision to comply with his demands rather than resist?'

'Yes.'

'Did you scream? Cry out?'

'No. I was afraid.'

'I see. Have you ever been held up before?'

'No.'

'Have you ever given money away?'

'Yes, of course.'

'And you did so willingly?'

'What are you getting at?'

'Well, let's put it like this, Mr Smith. You've given money

away in the past. In fact you have quite a reputation for philan-thropy. How can we be sure you weren't *contriving* to have your money taken by force?'

'Listen, if I wanted …'

'Never mind. What time did this hold-up take place?'

'About 11 p.m.'

'You were out on the street at 11 p.m? Doing what?'

'Just walking.'

'Just walking? You know that it's dangerous being out on the street that late at night. Weren't you aware that you could have been held up?'

'I hadn't thought about it.'

'What were you wearing?'

'Let's see – a suit. Yes, a suit.'

'An *expensive* suit?'

'Well – yes. I'm a successful lawyer, you know.'

'In other words, Mr Smith, you were walking around the streets late at night in a suit that practically advertised the fact that you might be a good target for some easy money, isn't that so? I mean, if we didn't know better, Mr Smith, we might even think that you were *asking* for this to happen, mightn't we?'

So goes an excerpt from a handbook issued by the London Rape Crisis Centre in 1984. A neat send-up of a lawyer's line of questioning of rape complainants, it ridicules attitudes that are long gone. Right?

Not necessarily. Just six months before Justin's trial, Andrew Lovett, the only AFL footballer ever to face charges of rape, found himself before a jury. He hired David Grace, a QC, to defend him. Like David Galbally, Grace was a 'footy lawyer,' a legal counsel for the West Coast Eagles who had represented individual players, such as Carlton's former captain Chris Judd, at the AFL's own in-house tribunal.

During the Lovett trial Grace asked the complainant about the length of her skirt. 'Was the skirt a short miniskirt? Was it a skirt that went from the waist down to your thighs? Did it start at your waist or below your waist? … Was there any flesh visible between the end of the singlet and the top of the skirt? … What was the distance between the top of the skirt and the bottom of the skirt?'

He asked if she intended to wear the clothes she did that night to 'make yourself look attractive' and, 'That night you were interested in meeting young men, is that right?' Not once did anyone in the courtroom point out that a woman may dress attractively – yes, to attract, but also to expand her *choice* of potential partners rather than to 'invite' unwanted sex.

At one stage of the questioning, the complainant tried to defend herself but it was as if she had accepted Grace's logic: 'I've never had a one-night stand in my life and if I was intending on that, wouldn't I have worn a G-string instead of a Bonds pair of undies?' she said.

Whether the woman had one-night stands and what she was wearing were not on trial; decades of rape awareness education and law reform have sought to do away with such assumptions. But it is as if many defence lawyers can't quite give up the ghost of this line of questioning despite knowing it ought not factor in a rape investigation – it is just too good an opportunity to appeal to the lowest common denominator on the jury.

\*

In his questioning, Malcolm Thomas also ticked off the lowest common denominators.

Did you scratch him?

Did you try biting him?

Did you punch out at him at all?

Did you hit out at him at all?

He asked about seeing Nate on the street after the alley, when Sarah waited with Justin for a cab. He asked if she said anything to him.

At this, Ryan sprang to his feet, asking to discuss the matter without the jury present. Taft agreed. Once the jury was dismissed, the judge turned to Thomas.

'Mr Thomas,' he said, 'in re-examination the Crown could make an application to lead evidence as to why she might not be seeking help from Nate. I don't know what she will say, but there may well be something which would ventilate the very issues which we have all been at pains to avoid.'

The jury was brought back in and Thomas continued. He asked Sarah about the height of her heels, how much alcohol she had consumed and the logistics of a man raping a much taller woman without any physical scuffle. Like a form of product placement, he dropped in the words 'lie' and 'lying' throughout his cross-examination. 'Can I suggest to you …' he began, as if he were simply offering Sarah alternative realities rather than trying to catch her out. He asked her about the alleys she had looked at with the police, about her slight delay in identifying the one that the prosecution was now claiming to be *the* alleyway. Was this, he hinted, because the police door-knock had produced a potential witness in this previously overlooked alley?

Was identifying this alley a matter of convenience rather than reality, akin to forcing pieces of a puzzle to fit?

It was an insinuation Ryan took issue with later in the trial. 'There is an issue that is floating around as a consequence of these questions,' he complained to Taft. 'There's the coppers put Ms Wesley up to what eventuated … it's floating around here at the moment and about when things are happening and what things are happening and the old saying about "prepared to wound but not to kill" comes to mind.'

'Prepared to wound but not to kill' – surely a tried and true adage for many defence lawyers in a sexual assault case? To pick at the seams of an allegation, to create doubt without going too far and annihilating the complainant, and thereby eliciting a juror's sympathy for her. But apart from these murky insinuations of doubt, there were actual discrepancies. As Thomas had said in his opening address, phone records don't lie – and contrary to what the jury had been told, Sarah's phone records revealed that there were no calls to Shaw from her phone until 7.16 a.m. Thomas added that she had paid the taxi driver outside her college just four minutes earlier.

Not only that, but Shaw had been trying to get in touch with her. He had even sent a text message offering to pick her up around the time she exited the alley on Dorcas Street. If Sarah had been trying so hard to contact him, Thomas intimated, then why didn't she just answer his calls? And if she didn't receive them, then why did her phone suddenly work when she and Justin exchanged numbers, she reciting her number to him and he calling her so that she could record his number. *In-te-rest-ing*, you could almost hear Thomas say, an eyebrow raised at the jury.

And it was interesting. Why did Sarah's phone records tell a different story? What reason would Sarah have to say otherwise? Was it because she thought her behaviour was confusing, not only to police but also to Justin, to Tom and perhaps even to herself?

Thomas continued to wound. He suggested to Sarah that others had seen her be affectionate with Justin in the street. There were witnesses who had seen them leave the house together. And again, Ryan later took issue with this. Sarah was the foreigner in this world, he said, the outsider, and whatever evidence was at odds with her version was a result of something sinister. A conspiracy of mates. As Thomas ticked off his lowest common denominators, so too did Ryan. Justin was a footballer, he had mates, and you know what that means.

But in a sense both Sarah and Justin were outsiders. In the long list of witnesses called to give evidence, only two were friends of Justin, and only two friends of Sarah. As for Nate Cooper, Justin knew him only vaguely, just enough to be his friend on Facebook.

Justin was on the fringes. And this was why he was interesting. Yes, he had a foot in the football fraternity, especially now that his former teammate was an A-grade player, but he was also an unremarkable young man in an ordinary world. There was no club drawing him to its protective flank. He was not on his own as Sarah was that night, but he wasn't part of the inner circle. Even in the bedroom, he was on the fringes. A lurker, not a player. Outsiders and insiders were not always so easily distinguished – as the case of Andrew Lovett showed.

# CHAPTER 12

In 2009, Christmas Eve morning, Andrew Lovett, an indigenous player, was alleged to have raped a woman on the bed of his St Kilda teammate, Jason Gram, after a night of drinking at a pub in Richmond. The woman and her friend had returned to the apartment with Lovett and Gram.

The alleged victim had been kissing Gram, but was so drunk that she was put on his bed to sober up. In court, the friend gave evidence that she had tried to take the woman home, but she was a dead weight. The friend said she grabbed her by the ankles and tugged. In slurred speech, the woman said, 'I can't move.'

The friend left the bedroom, and Gram and the woman kissed. Lovett was then said to have come into the room and implored Gram not to let the girls leave: 'Don't let them leave yet, don't let them leave.' Gram testified that he then left the room and joined the friend on the balcony.

Some fifteen, twenty minutes later, three more players arrived from the pub, and from here everything seemed to happen at once. The new arrivals saw the woman slumped against the wall in the hallway, crying. One player stepped over her to see 'what the boys were up to' and grab a beer from the fridge. Another shouted, 'What the fuck is going on with this chick crying at the front door?'

Gram and the woman's friend emerged from the balcony. The woman's friend said that she went to the bedroom first, only to find Lovett in there. 'He just kind of stared at me,' she said. 'It was just a weird look.' In the hallway, she found her friend curled up in a ball and crying. 'He fucked me. He fucked the shit out of me,' the woman eventually said, 'the dark guy.' She was heard to say to Gram, 'I feel like a slut. I thought it was you.' Her friend later testified that the woman had whimpered to her, 'I was asleep, you know. I said no.'

When the woman tried to call her ex-boyfriend, struggling to tell him where she was, one player took the phone from her and told the person at the other end of the line the address.

After the woman left the apartment, the players said they crowded around Lovett, trying to find out what had happened. St Kilda's ruckman, Adam Pattison, told the court, 'I remember Fisher saying, "Did you chop her?" and Lovett said, "Yeah, I did, but she had no problem."' Another player told Lovett to 'fuck off and that he wasn't wanted at St Kilda anymore.' 'How could you bring the club down like this?' said another.

Following Lovett outside, Jason Gram and his housemate, the player Sam Fisher, called him a 'dog.'

According to Gram, Lovett collapsed at that point and was in tears. 'Are you serious? This is bullshit,' he said.

Gram suggested they go back upstairs and make some calls. 'When something like this happens,' he explained to the jury, 'we normally have to call our football manager.'

Lovett refused. He later sent one of the players a text message. It read in part, 'Hey mate, as far as I'm concerned I thought we were OK to hook up … I feel terrible for her, but I am not the type!'

From that morning, Lovett had no contact with most of his teammates. It's believed that club officials at St Kilda told them not to associate with him. You could say this was an impressive instance of players standing up for a woman, but it's also true – albeit cynical – to note that Lovett was not yet bonded to this team. Having just been recruited to St Kilda, he hadn't even played a match with them.

As the prosecution later suggested, Lovett may have had a sense of entitlement to the woman, interpreting Gram leaving the bedroom as a kind of 'hand-pass,' but may not have realised that he was not yet 'one of the boys.'

The protective flank of the club was nowhere to be seen. This was entirely unlike what had happened with St Kilda players Stephen Milne and Leigh Montagna, both of whom were rallied by the widespread support they received when they were questioned for rape. Teammates and fans came out to wish the boys well. The coach, Grant Thomas, said to reporters then that the rape allegations could ultimately strengthen the club: 'I've got no doubt that it will galvanise us and make us even stronger and closer and better.' The club president, Rod Butterss, said that he felt 'absolutely empowered' as fans rallied around the Saints. St Kilda said Milne and Montagna had the right to be presumed innocent.

Lovett received no such support or presumption. He was immediately suspended and banned from group activities indefinitely. Twice a week he was required to complete a skills sessions with a development coach and run solo time-trials. After he was charged, St Kilda terminated his contract, a three-year deal worth more than $1 million.

So was Lovett's dismissal a sign of better times – that the league's hardline stance regarding its Respect & Responsibility policy has seen even the most rebellious of clubs fall into line – or was it just a lack of mates? And if the former, then confronting one problem has led to new issues. How to uphold certain standards while maintaining an individual's basic rights?

As the sports commentator Tim Lane wrote in the *Age*, Andrew Lovett represented 'the awkward issue of the fundamental right of the individual to be considered innocent until proven otherwise.'

There is also the reasonable question as to whether an AFL footballer is entitled to expect that his employer won't act precipitously in circumstances which might prejudice public opinion of him. For while the AFL and its clubs are public institutions whose reputations are vital to their success – hence the 'bringing the game into disrepute' clause – so too are the players judged by the public. They, too, are entitled to reasonable protection of their professional and personal reputations.

The AFL is a 'juggernaut that is a law unto itself,' said the outspoken criminal defence lawyer Rob Stary when the Geelong Cats banned a player from senior selection for the rest of the 2012 season after police were called to his home to investigate an allegation of domestic assault. The Players Association agreed, and feared such a penalty could prejudice the footballer's case.

A statement by the AFL applauded the Cats' decision, in words that implied guilt. 'With this sanction, the Geelong Football Club and its leadership group have sent a powerful message to the AFL industry and the community more broadly that violence against women is never acceptable,' said Adrian Anderson, the league's general manager at the time. 'The AFL's Respect & Responsibility policy is very clear that inappropriate player behaviour will not be tolerated ...'

Both football codes now find themselves in a no-win situation, damned by critics if they act and damned if they don't. In the NRL, when a star player for the Manly Sea Eagles, Brett Stewart, was charged with sexual assault in 2009, his team's board decided – after a meeting that took them well past midnight – that Stewart could continue playing. The decision was met with bristling anger from commentators. Peter FitzSimons, a former Wallaby player and now writer, told ABC's *Lateline*:

> In the realm of the bleeding obvious, it doesn't get much more bleeding obvious than that. Stewart should not play on Saturday night. And that's not to judge his innocence or his guilt; it's to say there are serious matters that need to be resolved and until such times as they are resolved, you won't play, you won't wear our proud jersey.

The league's own sexual assault adviser, Karen Willis of the NSW Rape Crisis Centre, agreed, while the state's premier, Nathan Rees, said simply, 'The decision of Mr Stewart to be allowed to play this weekend should be reviewed by Manly. It sends entirely the wrong messages.'

The club remained resolute while the league struggled to find its position on the matter, tiptoeing through a moral quagmire: how to uphold the NRL's newfound standards while not pre-empting judgment of Stewart?

The NRL then decided to suspend the star fullback for four rounds. The club and his teammates were up in arms, but the league insisted the suspension was actually imposed to punish Stewart for his drunkenness at the club's season launch, an event which preceded the alleged sexual assault.

Stewart was eventually acquitted of the assault charges. Andrew Lovett, too, was found not guilty. He walked free from his trial but despite his attempts to get redrafted into the AFL, his playing career was effectively over.

*

How to balance the two imperatives? Without suspension, penalties, dismissal and some act of acknowledgment, what can complainants take comfort from? How to avoid the endless victory photos in the press, players carried on the shoulders of their teammates, the news coverage, the TV footage, the roar of the crowd, the lit-up night as floodlights stream from stadiums, chanting of football fans spilling onto the streets, even the blue glow of TV screens on your own street? A complainant may want to be sick, dead even, among all this. Knowing that certain players – now focused on the ball as intently as they were on her – are the source of all this adoration, that she is dismissed as nothing more than an off-field distraction.

And yet an eagerness to judge is a dangerous thing. Just as the myth of the 'deserving' rape victim persists – a woman who is drunk is more likely to be seen to be 'asking for it' – a fixed image of footballers and male athletes as badly behaved jocks and potential rapists is also beginning to take shape.

In the spring of 2006 in North Carolina, allegations that a young black woman was raped, sodomised, robbed and strangled by members of the Duke University lacrosse team mobilised the left-liberal members of the university faculty and grabbed the attention of the US media.

Known as 'the group of 88,' professors and affiliates at the university signed a full-page advertisement (although the academics involved preferred to call it a 'listening statement') and published it in the college's daily newspaper less than two weeks after a woman was hired to strip at a party organised by the team's captains, where she said she had been raped.

'What Does a Social Disaster Sound Like?' the headline read. It continued:

> We are listening to our students … Regardless of the results of the police investigation, what is apparent every day now is the anger and fear of many students who know themselves to be objects of racism and sexism, who see illuminated in this moment's extraordinary spotlight what they live with everyday … These students are shouting and whispering about what happened to this young woman and to themselves.

Residents, students and faculty members – upset with the team members' silence and the university's handling of the case –

staged five protests in four days, while activists handed out WANTED posters with pictures of the team. One professor, Houston Baker, established himself as a 'leading dissident voice' on campus, and issued a public letter to the university administration two weeks after the allegations – a period which he called one of 'silent protectionism.'

> How is a Duke community citizen to respond to such a national embarrassment from under the cloud of a 'culture of silence' that seeks to protect white, male, athletic violence and which apparently prevents all university citizens from even surveying the known facts? …
>
> The lacrosse team – 15 of whom have faced misdemeanor charges for drunken misbehavior in the past three years – may well feel they can claim innocence and sport their disgraced jerseys on campus, safe under the cover of silent whiteness. But where is the black woman who their violence and raucous witness injured for life? Will she ever sleep well again?

Although Duke University cancelled the remainder of the lacrosse season and the coach was forced to resign, it was not enough for Baker.

> There can be no confidence in an administration that believes suspending a lacrosse season and removing pictures of Duke lacrosse players from a web page is a dutifully moral response to abhorrent sexual assault, verbal racial violence, and drunken white male privilege loosed among us.

The media then took up the baton and ran with it. On CNN, Wendy Murphy said, 'Look, I think the real key here is that these guys, like so many rapists – and I'm going to say it because, at this point, she's entitled to the respect that she is a crime victim. These guys watch *CSI*, they know it's a really bad idea to ejaculate on or in the victim.'

*Newsweek* magazine plastered mug shots of the boys on its cover. Headlines hollered 'Duke lacrosse rape case' and 'Gang Rape Case.' Many in the media took the words of the prosecutor, Michael Nifong, as gospel. He told reporters that the lacrosse team was sticking together in a conspiracy of silence, and lo and behold, Johnette Howard, a columnist at *Newsday*, wrote:

> There's something disgustingly wrong when a Duke University
> men's lacrosse team … puts some skewed code of silence ahead
> of telling Durham, N.C., police everything they know.

But it wasn't true. The team was talking to police and all players were complying with DNA tests, minus the team's one black player, who was never implicated. They had even offered to take polygraph tests.

Three players were charged, banned from setting foot on campus and, for the year that they faced accusations, used constantly as examples of privileged jocks by an insatiable media. But the sexual assault allegations, it turned out, were false – disastrously so.

Twice, DNA tests found no matches. The prosecutor, Nifong, misleadingly claimed that this was not unusual. Worse, when the defence cross-examined the DNA expert, he said that Nifong had persuaded him to withhold evidence from authorities that while the DNA of several men was found on the complainant, none matched that of the Duke players.

The police line-ups were also curated by Nifong, with only photos of the lacrosse players provided for the complainant to choose from, unlike in standard line-ups where suspects are mixed in with others – it was a 'multiple-choice test in which there were no wrong answers,' as the defence lawyers put it. Even so, it was only on the third occasion that, with obvious uncertainty, the complainant picked out three of the young men. To top it all off, a second stripper who had performed at the party said there was no rape, later telling *60 Minutes* that the allegations were a 'crock.'

Nifong was eventually disbarred over his conduct and later charged with criminal contempt – he spent one day in jail. The Durham police also came under fire for allowing Nifong to act as a kind of de facto head of investigation. A year later, when the case was finally dropped, the new prosecutor took the unusual step of clearing the men's names. He said he did not just find 'insufficient evidence,' but declared the three players were innocent, that no rape had occurred, a 'rogue prosecutor' had not been reined in, and that 'in the rush to condemn, a community and a state lost the ability to see clearly.'

Stephen Baldwin, a professor of chemistry at Duke University, summed it up nicely: 'There was a collision between political correctness and due process, and political correctness won.' It seemed that alongside that of the slut, the stereotype of the vicious, stupid and pampered jock was gaining momentum.

The Duke University president later apologised for 'causing the families to feel abandoned when they most needed support.'

But what ought he do in the future? Even when the university did the 'right thing' – suspending the lacrosse season and the indicted players – these symbolic gestures were not enough. Must we leapfrog from one stereotype to another? Provide scalps for a baying public? Surely the first thing one ought to do is distinguish what exactly the athletes were being tried for – was it for gang rape, or for being privileged white male athletes?

\*

When I took my seat again in the courtroom, the screen above the witness stand was black. Opaque. The feeling in the room was different. The jurors' eyes were bright. They were sitting up straight. Sarah had given her testimony. Everything about the space was more charged, electric. In the far back corner, however, was a weight. Justin seemed smaller, deflated, as if the air had been sucked out of him. The trial had only just begun, but he was exhausted. Ashen, he had turned the colour of the city streets, of the cigarette smoke on the courthouse steps.

# CHAPTER 13

In the heat, the blisters and Band-Aids on my feet from wearing nice shoes chafed. Court had finished for the day, and with a slight limp I headed for the train station. On autopilot, I crossed the streets at the lights, turning the trial over in my head. Then suddenly, deep in thought, I found myself bowing as if I was still in the courtroom and the passers-by were judges. I looked around sheepishly to check if anyone had seen me.

My thoughts were occupied with Sarah – or better, occupied with her absence, the empty seats behind the prosecution. Three times I had tried to contact her – through her lawyers, the police and her Facebook page – each attempt more panicky as I grew closer to Justin and his family. I had received no response. I tried again, pleaded with Sarah to let me know if she did not want to talk, but there was nothing.

I desperately did not want to replace Sarah with myself – to use a younger version of myself as a stand-in and my own experiences to explain hers.

And I'm hard on her, that younger version of me. I was too compliant, too inarticulate. Would this make me tough on Sarah?

Was my judgment warped by my own experiences? Was it dangerous to write about this trial when Sarah was not present in court, let alone speaking to me?

Would I fill her absence with my own reflection?

And what about her, how did she perceive her absence? Sure, she had appeared by remote camera, the jury had seen her – but she wasn't *here*.

\*

*Can you finish me off?* It kept coming back to me, the familiarity of it. It summed up the flipside of a night that started off with wanting and being wanted and ended in being treated like a cum rag. And yet it was a question, wasn't it? One you could say no to. That is, if you still had a voice, a solid sense of self. Perhaps there was a struggle in the alley, but is it possible the struggle was internal? What happened in the house – whatever side of the law it fell on – had seen the ground fall out from beneath Sarah's feet. Was it conceivable that she had entered that bedroom a woman and left an object, an alchemical reaction from which Justin later reaped the benefits? Had she accepted – internalised – the objectification of her?

People talk about sex and power as if power is a seesaw, divvied up between two people. But in night games, where you come up against the power of a group, your sense of self dislocates. Power here can come in the form of a magnetism where no obvious violence, force or even threats are necessary. You just end up moving accordingly. Obediently.

Savannah Dietrich, the Kentucky teenager who outed her

attackers on Twitter, was an anomaly. Before the trial she suffered enormously: suicide, she said, seemed a 'friendly option' and she cried herself to sleep. She was sixteen years old at the time of the assault, and her high school became a site of humiliation. She had no idea who or how many people had seen and passed on the photos of her unconscious, semi-undressed and being assaulted. But after going to the police – something she said she would not have done if the boys had apologised and told her, as she had asked, the names of the people they had shown the photos to – she summoned a rare strength that saw her not only choose to attend the trial but also to confront her attackers directly, speaking to them and trying to look them in the eye – something they avoided – when she gave evidence.

In a sense, Dietrich became empowered. Her presence during the trial made her unforgettable and indelible in the proceedings. The teenagers who assaulted her could not just walk away from her as they had that evening. Instead, they had to wear her presence, feel her anger and suffering, have her witness their shame as they had witnessed hers. If she had been absent, it would have been far easier for them to dismiss her as a 'bitch' or a 'slut' – and likewise, if she had avoided them, they could have loomed larger than life in her mind, morphed into monsters, young men with no chinks, no vulnerabilities. But instead she saw them broken, 'damaged goods' even – and herself as, in part, repaired.

Of course, it helped that her attackers pleaded guilty. Her word was not on trial. But still, by allowing Sarah to give evidence via remote camera, a screen that didn't even include a sight-line to Justin in the dock, was this as helpful or protective as reformers had hoped it would be?

Instead it seemed to sustain any one-dimensional and dehumanised images the complainant and defendant might have of each other – and in essence, to make a trial only about its end result, not a process.

But the alternative would mean having to look your accused attacker in the eye. And it would also mean having to look your alleged victim in the eye.

On early Monday morning, when Sarah was due to continue giving her evidence, the location where she was to be hooked up 'experienced technical difficulties.' The only solution was to use the remote camera facilities in the County Court, where the trial was. Somewhere in the same building, she was to be placed in front of a camera and streamed into court – but the proceedings kept being put off.

How to get Sarah into the County Court without her crossing paths with Justin?

'She dropped like a stone,' a court volunteer had told me of a similar scenario. A woman coming to court to give evidence found herself in the same lift as her attacker. Each of them was flanked by lawyers and supporters, and one party had rushed to get in the lift before the doors shut. It was too late when they all realised the mistake, and as the lift elevated, she fell to the ground.

Is this what I am pushing for?

It seems heinous and cruel to suggest that a victim go through this – experience their attacker's power over them again and again. But at the same time, I can't help thinking that in certain cases something is lost, a truth is unseen, without a negotiated meeting of some sort.

'Why is she doing this?' Justin's girlfriend Vanessa had asked me outside court when Justin went to the bathroom. It took me a moment to realise she was talking about Sarah. I paused.

'Because she's angry,' I said finally.

Vanessa didn't say anything, so I kept talking. 'I mean, she was treated badly that night. I don't know if she was raped, but even if she wasn't, she's got a reason to be angry.'

Vanessa looked at me in surprise, as if she had not contemplated my trying to see things through Sarah's eyes. She moved away. When Justin emerged, his family looked at him, as they did each time he returned from the bathroom, checking to see if he was okay.

I tried to imagine Sarah here in the foyer, alongside the Dyer family, having to walk the gauntlet of their accusing eyes. I pictured her in the bathroom and glancing in the mirror as Justin's mother or girlfriend walked in. And so too for Justin – he would have to withstand the rage and hate emanating from her supporters. It would hardly be pleasant. But at the same time, I thought, why were we all here, people who could never know for certain what happened in the alley, when one of the protagonists – one of the only two who did know – wasn't? Maybe if Sarah and Justin saw each another again, each broken and angry, they might be able to admit something to themselves and negotiate a common truth that so far had not been forced to surface.

\*

Could restorative justice play a part in dealing with sexual assault? Justice Marcia Neave thinks it could. A former chair of the Victorian Law Reform Commission, Neave oversaw substantial reform of sexual assault laws and yet remained disappointed at their limited effect on reporting and conviction rates. Speaking to the *Age* in 2011, she expressed her concern at the 'very, very low' conviction rates for sexual assault. Wrote journalist Farah Farouque: 'These have fallen in recent years, from a conviction in about 50 per cent of cases that went to trial in the County Court to 38 per cent in 2009–10; in addition, guilty pleas have plummeted, and the number of victims who report sexual offences to the police is less than 20 per cent.'

Others, such as the barrister Peter Morrissey, have expressed frustration at sexual assault cases clogging up the courts in spite of the very low chance of conviction. 'People are encouraged to want more out of the judicial system than what it offers,' he told the ABC's *7.30 Report* in 2008.

Justice Neave has proposed an alternative of 'restorative justice,' whereby the complainant and defendant attend a conference chaired by an independent person to discuss the offence, its effect on the complainant and how redress could be sought. Restorative justice has the ambitious goal of *changing* the offender while also meeting the needs of the complainant.

It is a controversial suggestion, one that carries the risk of 're-victimising' the complainant, with the offender able to excercise power over his victim once again, and one that may initially appear to feminists as a step backwards to a time when domestic violence and sexual assault were seen as lesser crimes and not taken seriously in court.

Yet the reflex objection that an offender is not being sufficiently punished if the case goes to a restorative justice conference instead of to court is superficial. After all, more often than not the accused leaves court in much the same physical state as they arrived: free. And if truly guilty, the offender is unaware of the impact of their crime and runs the risk of reoffending. On the other hand, an offender may find the process of having to speak to their victim much more difficult than sitting in court and leaving the talking to their barrister.

However, Justice Neave was well aware such a process would not suit all cases, emphasising that restorative justice would work alongside – not replace – the criminal justice system. But, she told the *Age*, she had spoken to many sexual assault victims over the years who were less concerned with retribution than they were with being acknowledged by their attacker and the system.

'They want a voice in the process,' said Neave. In an evaluation study, she quoted a woman who said, 'I just wanted some sort of validation, someone to say, "Yes, it happened," or for him to say, "Yes, it happened," and then I would have been fine.'

Could this have worked for Sarah and Justin?

It was hard to tell, perhaps because their positions had solidified in the course of the criminal justice process. Justin was adamant he had done nothing wrong, while Sarah was convinced of his guilt – and one couldn't help but wonder, whatever the trial's outcome, if either party would emerge any the wiser.

# PART 3
# THE WINMAR MOMENT

# CHAPTER 14

To this day, football codes around the world hold their post-game interviews in the locker room – and if footy is the last bastion of masculinity, then the locker room is the inner sanctum.

In America, when a Federal Court ordered equal locker-room access for female journalists in 1978, hostility towards women seemed merely to strengthen. Female reporters were accidentally 'locked out,' snubbed, called 'perverts' (while being slapped on the bum with wet towels) and subjected to numerous 'jokes' such as players urinating in front of them.

For the most part, the 'fending off intruders' approach worked. Unable to do their jobs properly and in the face of constant intimidation, few women stayed in sports journalism. But then, in 1990, came a watershed moment. Covering the US National Football League, a *Boston Herald* sports reporter, Lisa Olson, was trying to interview a footballer. She had requested for the interview to be held somewhere private, but the player insisted she meet him in the locker room. In hindsight, his response led Olson to suspect a concerted effort to intimidate her was planned.

As she began the interview, she heard another player call out, 'She's here again,' and then a group of players, all naked, stood around her. One fondled himself, held his dick out and said, 'Here's what you want. Do you want to take a bite out of this?' The other players echoed him. Another stood behind her, gyrating. 'After a few minutes, I gave up trying to interview Maurice, thanked him and walked away. I felt total, blind rage,' she told *People* magazine. A subsequent investigation saw Olson describe how the players 'positioned themselves inches away from my face and dared me to touch their private parts.'

When Olson told her editor about the incident, she asked him to handle it quietly and diplomatically. This did not happen, and when a rival newspaper, the *Boston Globe*, ran a story on the incident, the owner of the New England Patriots, Victor Kiam, responded angrily. Kiam argued the *Boston Herald* had 'asked for trouble' by assigning a female reporter, and male news reporters overheard him calling Olson 'a classic bitch.' However, Kiam quickly went into damage control when women's organisations threatened a boycott of his company, Remington, which sold women's shaving products. He spent some $100,000 on full-page newspaper ads protesting his innocence, apologised to Olson and blamed the club administration for not briefing him properly.

Reluctantly, the US National Football League ordered an investigation into the incident after Olson, who described her experience as 'mind-rape,' brought a lawsuit. The investigation, which resulted in a 108-page report, concluded that Olson had been 'degraded and humiliated.' Fines were levied against the club and specific players (though a news report later revealed that the players' fines were never collected).

A 'watershed' moment for female journalists, yes – but for Olson, despite winning a civil suit, the personal toll was immeasurable. Fans urged her to kill herself, made obscene phone calls, and sent her death threats, threats to rape her and threats to throw battery acid in her face. Her apartment was burgled, perpetrators leaving a note ordering her to 'Leave Boston or die,' and her car tyres were slashed, with a note left on the windscreen threatening, 'The next time it will be your neck.' 'I can't eat, I can't sleep. It's ruined my life,' Olson told *People* magazine. When the *Boston Herald* offered her a transfer to Australia to work for the *Daily Telegraph*, she took it and fled.

*

Around the same time, Jacquelin Magnay was taking a similar stand. Before becoming a sports reporter at the *Sydney Morning Herald* in 1992, Magnay worked for a suburban paper, which included covering rugby league. 'I'd covered St George, where Roy Masters was the coach. He was very welcoming, the photographer and I [both females] we'd go to their training and be treated as journos, but then we'd go to Cronulla and we'd have to psych ourselves up in the car, telling ourselves that this week was going to be different, that we could do it, that we could withstand the stares, the snarls, the spitting. But we persisted. It took about a year of horrible experiences until the Cronulla coach relented and realised that we weren't going to go away. He started to invite us to talks and was very welcoming. But it took a year and I wouldn't wish that on anybody.'

Travelling back and forth with her notepad, Magnay had her fair share of good and bad teams to deal with. By the time she joined the *Sydney Morning Herald*, she was a seasoned hand at navigating the mixed receptions at rugby clubs. 'My reaction was to have no reaction. When I was interviewing the CEO of a club, one player got up on a table and started dancing in front of me naked. At Penrith, the coach had the press conference huddle standing in front of the showers, him facing us, so we would have to face the players in the showers. So I'd turn the coach around, so that we didn't have to look at them. Naked players sometimes sidled up behind you. When I look back on it, I think, oh my god, that was sexual harassment to the nth degree. It was uncomfortable, awkward and intimidating, and for other people in the room to find that acceptable, then shame on them. I was a young journalist and they allowed that to happen.'

Magnay pushed on. 'I'd established a protocol where I'd let the clubs know when I was attending their games, but my job was continually hindered by rugby league's Balmain Tigers [now the Sydney Tigers], then coached by Alan Jones. At one Balmain game I told the doorman at the dressing room to let officials know I was there, but either the message wasn't passed on or I was ignored. It meant that I missed the post-game interview and the opportunity to talk to the players, although I could talk to them an hour later when they came out of the rooms, but it was quite a time delay.' By that time, the reporters from rival papers had filed their stories.

Unhappy that she had missed the press conference, Magnay's editor wrote a letter of complaint to Balmain and organised with club management that the next time she was there, they would conduct the post-match interview outside the change rooms in the tunnel.

'God, you must have felt like a leper,' I interrupted.

'Yes,' Magnay said slowly. 'And also you have to imagine I was quite a young journalist, and to take on the very senior rugby guys – very established names in the industry – was not insignificant.'

The next Balmain game was in Newcastle and Magnay had given the club two days' notice she would be attending. 'So I get there after the game, standing outside in this dingy, dark, horrible tunnel, and everyone trots into the dressing room, including all male journalists, TV cameras, radio journalists. I knocked on the door and said, "Can you please let Alan know I'm outside?"' She waited about ten minutes, then as someone else went inside, she peered in and could see Alan Jones holding his press conference huddle. 'I called across the room and said, "Alan, I just want to let you know that I'm here. Can you please hold the press conference outside?"'

Jones stormed over to Magnay. 'He berated me, saying I was carrying on like a temperamental schoolgirl and what right did I have to be there.' Magnay stood her ground. As calmly as she could, she told Jones that she was taping everything he said. 'He said, "Turn the tape off," and I said, "No, everything you say is on the record." Then, quite remarkably, he did a complete 180-degree turn and started to hold the press conference in the tunnel.' By now Magnay was shaking, barely able to hear a word Jones said.

With the help of the media union, Magnay lodged a complaint with the Human Rights Commission. 'I wanted to get a legal framework for what I was doing and what other females were attempting to do, and that was to be able to do our jobs properly.' During the proceedings, a blood-spattered knife arrived in the mail for her. Several colleagues gave her the cold shoulder. 'Going into the dressing room was seen very much as going into the inner sanctum,' Magnay explained. 'It was a privileged position to be in: they had access to this secret world of male domain, and they wanted that to remain. They didn't want women there and they didn't want anything to happen where they couldn't get access.' Other male journalists, however, were supportive. 'A rival journalist actually helped me in the court case and filed supportive letters for me.'

Magnay's case was successful and made it illegal for national sporting clubs to discriminate against reporters on the basis of gender. The Tigers were forced to issue a public apology to her. But by then, Jones had left Balmain and taken up his post as a radio shock-jock. 'He continued to criticise me on his show.'

\*

Yet is entering the players' change room after a football match really a victory for equality, a coup for female sports journalists? Jason Whitlock on ESPN, the American sports media network, doesn't think so:

> A woman's opportunity to get to do the same dumb stuff that men do is not equality. You achieve equality when you share in the power and get to shape the rules and traditions so that they make sense for you.

When I put this to Magnay, she agreed. 'I have lobbied strongly with the NRL to interview the players in a mixed zone when they come off the field – after all, the radio guys have the chance to interview them on the field. We could have a chance, in the tunnel, or some way en route to the dressing room, to get quick quotes from the players after the game. But they never ever allowed that.'

In recent years, though, there have been changes. 'As the game is becoming more professional, it is becoming less of an insiders' club. Most journalists are now on the outer, you're not part of the inner sanctum anymore,' said Magnay. And the 'roll around in the same drip tray' relationship between male journalists and footy clubs, a relationship resembling to Magnay an endless Sunday barbeque, is less prevalent. 'Now, with immediacy, there isn't time for that.' Press conferences are held outside the change rooms, with coaches and captains sitting in front of sponsor-emblazoned banners. But journalists still go into the locker room to get comments from the players.

On ESPN, Whitlock described the feeding frenzy as a star player steps out of the shower and walks towards his locker:

> We, the media, will open up a walkway for the athlete to get his space, then crowd back around him and stand within 2 feet of him as he drops his towel and begins to undress.
>
> Somehow, we manage to cover wars and presidential campaigns and murder trials without going into sweaty filthy bathrooms for interviews ... Reporters can wax on about all their journalistic reasons to enter a locker room. It's bull ... a significant number of 'journalists' love going into the locker

room because it's something the average fan can't do. Makes
'em feel special, cool, important.

Football insiders dismissed female sports reporters as 'groupies,' but what they failed to acknowledge was that the locker
room had been frequented by groupies long before women were
allowed in.

'Talk about women being groupies, the men were outrageous,'
said Carlton's first female director, Lauraine Diggins, a fine arts
dealer and the daughter of Brighton Diggins, the Blues' 1938 premiership captain-coach. Her presence was a true feat considering
former president John Elliott's declaration that no woman would
make it onto the board at Carlton unless she'd played 100 games
of football. Diggins laughed as she recalled going into the locker
room after games. 'I used to treat going into the change rooms as
a job, but the men, they had this adoration. They were in awe of
the players. I had expectations, while they had adulation.'

And with this in mind, perhaps the likes of Alan Jones were
right. Women *were* intruders. Coming in from the outside like a
draft under the door, the presence of female reporters such as
Magnay in the inner sanctum broke a spell in this sweaty place
where players could do no wrong (and if they did, no one would
say a thing). Suddenly being worshipped may not have seemed
so much fun: being a god now came with responsibilities.

*

'What connection have *you* got to footy?' It is a question I was
asked often while researching this book – a question that women,

be they insiders or outsiders to the game, must continually confront.

'Well, I'm female, for starters,' I retorted defensively to one insider. The issues I was exploring, I continued, were as much about women as they were about footy. The reply worked – he went quiet – but I didn't like the implication, that I was writing this book for the sisterhood. Why did I have to explain myself? Surely the fact that I was a writer was enough?

When I was asked the question again – this time by a former player who then added that footy is just a game – I changed tack. This time I gave the hard-nosed journo response. Footy is big business, I said; its influence is vast. And it's not too difficult to make the connection between footy and power. Politicians, media moguls and businessmen – many of whom hail from an 'old boys' private school network – woo one another in corporate boxes, while league executives and star players take home million-dollar pay packages from a 'business' that, and here's the clanger, isn't taxed. Football clubs, football leagues, don't pay tax. Most sporting bodies don't. They are not-for-profit, so to speak, their status much like that of a charity. As the AFL's annual report explained in 2010, the league is exempt from income tax because its activities 'are solely the promotion, administration and development of Australian Rules Football.' The NRL's status is the same. Surely, I'd say, these perks must come with responsibilities? My foray into this world was an investigation like any other. I didn't *need* a connection to footy.

But still the questions continued.

A former player who now worked for the AFL asked me, with faux casualness, what team I followed. 'I like footy,' I started.

He let out an almost imperceptible sigh. People don't like football – they love it. 'But I do like it!' I said, frustrated. 'I like watching it on telly and having a kick in the park. But I don't come from a football family. I never had a team.' I paused as I scrambled for the words, and then found them: 'I grew up playing sport, not watching it.'

I was in two minds about being interrogated on my connection to football. On one hand, I resented it. It got my back up. Would a man be asked this question? But on the other hand, I was asking myself the same question. What was I doing here? What was any woman doing in this world of men? And why can't football be just a game? Why make more of it? Why ruin it with seedy accusations of a shadowy macho subculture, one that can just as easily be found in the military or even the construction industry, and then counter this with shrill claims that these men, boys, are heroes, 'role models'?

Nor was it hard to conclude that football had put itself at the mercy of a highly strung and self-righteous media. When CCTV footage of the former AFL player Brendan Fevola taking a piss in a shop alcove can be aired on Channel 7 and result in his club fining him $10,000, the codes do, at times, seem to be taking themselves too seriously. Then there was the $5000 fine imposed on Richmond's Matthew Richardson when he gave the finger to spectators, and the schoolmarmish, over-the-top posturing from journalists when Ben Cousins did the same to Channel Ten's remote-operated tilt-and-zoom camera installed in the change room (one might argue that cameras in the change room are over the top). Was I about to join this pious media chorus?

Over and over I asked myself this, especially when I watched a game on TV, singing 'shake down the thunder' for the Sydney Swans (my partner's team), watching in awe as Lewis Jetta, a lean Aboriginal player for the Swans, sprinted towards the goals while Collingwood players lumbered uselessly after him. Or laughing at the endless commentary about the seagulls that dotted the oval and bobbed in the air like a mobile, oblivious to the men pounding the turf.

The last thing I wanted to be was a killjoy – and yet I kept recalling the words of the Australian sociologist Lois Bryson. She once wrote that feminists who ignore sport do so at their own peril, and I couldn't shake the feeling that this was all the more true when it came to footy.

# CHAPTER 15

'I suggested that Denis might like to drop around to our home after a Sunday morning training session, have a coffee with us and tell our girls to their face how pathetic their gender was,' said Mary Crooks, cackling. It was 2005 and Carlton were down by seventy-seven points at half-time when their coach, Denis Pagan, lashed out at his players, calling them a bunch of 'schoolgirls and sheilas.'

A few days later, the back page of the *Herald Sun* carried the story. 'Pagan was alleged to have hurled all the abuse he could at his players for being in this terrible predicament at half-time,' recalled Crooks, 'and it seems the worst barb was to suggest they were playing like sheilas and schoolgirls. I had a flash of anger!' Crooks took to her computer and wrote Pagan a letter. She told him about her work at the Victorian Women's Trust, in particular overseeing an exhibition to mark 100 years of federation called *Ordinary Women, Extraordinary Lives.*

'Hundreds of women,' said Crooks, 'from all walks of life, doing the most amazing things – usually unheralded, unremunerated and most certainly not in football's Halls of Fame.' She wrote about how women's unpaid work was devalued and about her and her husband's two daughters. 'I wrote that we were intent on bringing them up to feel confident about themselves, filled with positive qualities and, importantly, wanting to be positive contributors to their society.'

Crooks then suggested Pagan come over for morning tea and tell her daughters that this upbringing was all for nothing, given their gender. Within a week, Crooks received a phone call from Pagan. She smiled, recalling the coach trying to make amends. 'He wriggled, squirmed and said that he sort of, had not really said what the *Herald Sun* had printed and that maybe he sort of, might have said that girls were not as physically strong as boys.'

'Poor Denis,' said Lauraine Diggins, who was at Carlton the same time as Pagan. 'He was so surprised, he had in no way intended to demean women. Footy was just so separate from the rest of the world. He learnt something that day.'

A couple of days after Pagan's call, Diggins phoned Crooks and told her that the Women of Carlton – the official female supporters group of the Blues – loved the letter. By the end of the month, Carlton's club president sent a formal invitation to Crooks asking if she would be interested in becoming one of the female ambassadors for the club. Crooks happily accepted.

\*

In the finer zoos of the world, species of animals are often added to the mix because they have a calming effect on the group as a whole. It's a strange idea but it does work. You don't fight the problem – you shift it by changing the power dynamic of the group.

So wrote Damien Foster, a professional mentor, in the *Age*, in light of the spate of sexual assault allegations against footballers – and slowly but surely the leagues and their clubs have been doing exactly that. Women are taking up jobs once offered only to men, support roles as fitness advisers, podiatrists, dieticians, physiotherapists, trainers, counsellors, public relations managers, sports scientists, umpires and referees.

Many of these appointments come with teething problems. Elaine Canty was appointed to the AFL tribunal in 1996. The tribunal is a curious scene with foldaway chairs, where players turn up in often ill-fitting suits with top-notch QCs or footy-tragic lawyers working for free for their favourite club, and where the jury might find itself watching a seven-second television grab of a controversial tackle for hours. When her role was announced, Canty was inundated with hate mail. A central objection – most notably from the legendary coach Ron Barassi – was that a woman couldn't do the job, having never played in the league. And it was true: the lawyer and broadcaster had never played professional football. But nor had the majority of the other members of the panel. This revelation produced an uncomfortable silence – no one had ever thought of asking the question of the tribunal's male members.

Speaking to the *AFL Record* in 1999, Canty emphasised why women needed to be represented in the league: 'It's an industry, whether we like to think so or not, and it has to be a reflection of women's place in the general community.' She added that these changes were not simply about wanting to be virtuous: 'I think they've [the AFL] made a cold-blooded commercial decision that it is in their interests to involve women in the administrative side of football.'

It certainly beats ragging out single mothers, as the league did in its 1994 report, blaming them for the decline in junior participation in the eighties: these over-anxious mothers were said to be steering their children away from footy and into sports they considered less dangerous, such as basketball and soccer. And it certainly makes up for the 5.7 million hours of unpaid work that 48,000 female volunteers contribute to the game annually. That's approximately $69 million in free labour, according to the AFL's calculations in 2003.

'The future of football is feminine,' announced the FIFA (Fédération Internationale de Football Association) boss Joseph Blatter in 1995 – and Australia's football codes caught on. The AFL is one of the few male-only sports codes in the world that can boast a large proportion of passionate female supporters. The columnist Chris Kenny did the maths in the *Australian*:

Men still dominate attendances, with Australian Bureau of Statistics figures from 2010 showing that 1.7 million males attended Aussie rules games compared with 1.2 million women. So female attendances are more than two-thirds the male number.

Rugby league, by comparison, had a million men attending and 600,000 women – something less than two-thirds. While the fractional differential is not large, when combined with the overall higher attendances it shows there are twice as many women attending Aussie rules as league.

In England, less than 15 per cent of those attending Premier League football are women. So you can see why the 'future is feminine' – what successful business would alienate half of its clientele?

Cue the NRL's 'To the Women in the League. We Salute You' campaign. Accompanied by the melodic tinkling of a piano, promotional footage shows selfless mothers painting white boundary lines on the oval, pumping up a football, stapling documents, hauling boxes of trophies from their cars, opening the cafeteria and attending to a player's leg injury.

Over the images a deep gravelly male voice says:

> This is dedicated to the unsung heroes who ask for nothing and give everything. You are the guardian angels, the gate-keepers, and the champion's champion, carrying the weight of thankless tasks with selfless hearts, you are the wind beneath our winners, the goddesses of war and peace, the patron saints of the sideline, the canteen queens who wear a beanie like a crown, you are the dream makers [camera flashes to little boy wearing footy jumper] who understand that greatness is not born, it is earned and easily squandered. You sculpt lives of greatness out of grass and dirt and mud, you don't seek fame or glory, but know this – our victories are your victories.

Excuse me while I vomit.

Are we changing stereotypes here or simply reinforcing them? With soppy advertisements like this one, it would be easy to *keep* seeing women as mere service providers. You have the mothers who cheer from the sidelines, drive to and from games and training, cook carbohydrates the night before, volunteer in the canteen and scrub the grass stains out of uniforms; women idolising their 'boys' who can do no wrong. Then there's the female support staff tending to the players' injuries, massaging their hamstrings, studying their eating habits and micro-managing their media image.

These are the 'good' women – or, as Kevin Sheedy and Carolyn Brown wrote in their book, the 'forgotten heroes.'

Oh, and let's not forget the WAGs, the tail of the dog. Otherwise known as 'wives and girlfriends' of footballers, they are expected not only to take over the reins from Mum, but to look hot too. They are service providers *and* trophies (and at the other end of the spectrum is the player who wins the wooden spoon for picking up the 'ugliest chick'). In the *Herald Sun*: 'Every sport has them, their stars wouldn't perform as well without them ... Take a look.' On radio: 'Triple M makes a calendar of Melbourne's Hottest WAGs!'

When three Brisbane Broncos players found themselves under investigation for claims of sexual assault at a nightclub, where they said they'd engaged in consensual sexual acts with a woman in a toilet cubicle (one of the men had filmed it on his mobile phone and phoned another player, saying, 'Guess what's happening inside here?'), the *Daily Telegraph* thought it relevant not only to note that one rugby player had 'lost his girlfriend Emma Harding' as a result of the incident, but also to link to a photo gallery titled 'Bronco Stunner Emma Harding.'

And amazingly, Wayne 'the King' Carey's fall from grace in the AFL came not after he grabbed a woman's breasts on a city street and told her, 'Why don't you get a bigger pair of tits?'

Nor was it when it came to light that his North Melbourne club had negotiated a $15,000 settlement with a woman who claimed to have been sexually harassed by Carey and another AFL player. Nor when he provided a character reference in court for the drug dealer and gangster Jason Moran, who was later murdered in Melbourne's gang war. No, Carey hit an all-time low in the popularity stakes in 2002 when he shagged teammate and vice-captain Anthony Stevens' wife in a bathroom at a party.

Touchingly, the Kangaroo players publicly linked arms around their vice-captain and Carey was shunned. But the issue wasn't about morality – if it had been, Carey would have been shunned years earlier. It was about propriety and betraying a teammate.

While I understand that employing more female support staff helps chip away at an entrenched and blinkered male society, and that the presence of professional females can help to re-humanise women in the eyes of these young men, it's the absence of females at the two most powerful ends of football that stands out: at the top and on the oval.

There is gender imbalance and there is power imbalance. And without fixing the latter, the former will continue to stink of servitude.

\*

In 1993, Beverly Knight became the first woman to be appointed to an AFL club board. She was also the longest-serving female director, only stepping down from her role at Essendon seventeen years later. 'It wasn't easy,' Knight said, as we sat in her art gallery in Melbourne's Fitzroy, huge indigenous works lighting up the walls around us. 'It was a real shock, I'd gone to a girls' school, I was my own boss.' For the first three years, Knight had to push herself constantly, often waking up with dread on the morning of a meeting.

'There were times I just didn't want to go to meetings or events, didn't want to face the snubs or the silences.' At events, Knight often found men turning their backs to her or relegating her to 'wife' status. She smiled: 'And another thing I had to deal with was that everyone was so tall.'

One of the most difficult doors to unlock in the football realm has been that to the boardroom – which is not surprising considering how much it resembles the rest of corporate Australia. Nominations to boards have traditionally relied on old boys' networks. One might assume this is because the clubs were running perfectly well – no need to fix something that isn't broken – but when Knight arrived at Essendon, the club was in dire financial straits.

'They were still running it like a local footy club,' she recalled, 'and I discovered they didn't have a members' department. It was crazy. They saw members as complainers rather than a cash cow.' In the first year of Knight's placement, she oversaw a jump in membership numbers from 10,000 to 25,000. Soon other clubs began to take an interest in what Essendon was doing, and Knight began to meet with them to discuss the importance of members.

Being a woman also saw Knight having to bring up the most ridiculous issues. When the MCG, Melbourne's main sports stadium, underwent a massive multi-million-dollar redevelopment, the new change-room sections were built without female toilets. 'Female staff had to share the disabled toilet,' Knight recalled wryly. 'When you're bringing it up, you sound absolutely pathetic in a roomful of men.'

And what about the locker room, I asked.

She sighed, shrugging in resignation, as if she had started out with one conviction but had to yield to another. 'I didn't go to the change rooms for the first six years and my advice to any female newcomer would be to go there immediately. It's the inner sanctum. But at the same time, I believe the players need privacy, not only from women, but from men. In those days so many men just hung around them all the time.'

Knight's main interest was promoting indigenous issues in the club and the league. Before her arrival on the board she was already sponsoring, among others, Michael Long, a young Essendon recruit who was soon to become one of the game's best and most influential players.

Smiling, Knight recalled a conversation with Long after she was nominated to Essendon's board. 'When I became the first female director, Michael telephoned me and said, "You're about to find out what it is like to be Aboriginal."'

Knight pushed hard for club selectors to consider more indigenous players, discovering that many were being dismissed, not because they weren't good enough, far from it, but because their situation, background and isolation from mainstream society were thought to be too hard to navigate. Across the code, Knight actively promoted indigenous players and fought stereotypes that Aboriginal players would muck up and drink too much, and that their families would humbug for money.

Today, both the AFL and Essendon Football Club are incredibly proud of their connection to indigenous Australia – and rightfully so. You could say that Beverly Knight, the first woman allowed into the code's engine room, was a key person behind one of the proudest achievements of the AFL and Essendon.

Yet Knight's contribution to the game didn't seem to register at her final board meeting. She proposed a quota system for women on the board, beginning at 30 per cent in a voluntary capacity over three to four years, and then to be mandated. 'I got stonewalled.' Knight shook her head, recalling how some members had said her proposal was no more than tokenism. Knight looked at me, her shoulders dropping, as if to say, 'What, there are no worthy women? Only tokens?'

*

In the past decade, the two football codes have made a concerted effort to have women directors and commissioners. In 2005, both the AFL and NRL appointed the first women to their governing bodies. Katie Page, the CEO of retail giant Harvey Norman, joined rugby league's executive board, while the former IAG Group executive Sam Mostyn joined the AFL's commission. Then in 2008, Linda Dessau, a family court judge, joined Mostyn at the AFL.

What about the clubs? When the high-powered businesswoman Lynn Ralph was appointed to the board of the Sydney Swans in 2007, she noted drily: 'I was the first woman. It was pretty embarrassing that there we were in the twenty-first century with no females on the board, and 40 per cent of the members were female.'

Today the AFL has eighteen female club directors, occupying close to 15 per cent of the board seats. The NRL has ten women on club boards. But despite it being the twenty-first century, as Ralph pointed out, many men still yearn for the good old days.

In 2003, the then vice-president of Melbourne Football Club, Beverley O'Connor, was told not to attend the club's annual Past & Present Players function. O'Connor, who had been in her role at the club for five years, was reported to have taken the snub with 'good grace,' while the invitation promised the 250 male attendees a 'good old-fashioned pie night just like the ones we used to have.'

In some quarters the presence of women in powerful positions has strengthened resentment, especially when they actually speak up. One former board member told me of enquiries she had made into confusing balance sheets. When she asked about the hefty amount of cash under the tag 'Maintenance,' she received 'opaque' and 'aggressive' responses from the male directors.

'What kind of maintenance costs this much, I wanted to know,' she told me, raising her eyebrow.

'Hush money?' I asked.

She raised her eyebrow a little higher and smiled. 'Well, I put an end to that kind of budget-keeping.'

'They serve very little purpose at board level,' said Sam Newman on *The Footy Show*, after five female club directors had written to complain about the 2008 episode that humiliated journalist Caroline Wilson. 'What do they do? I'm not knocking women [but] for very little input they demand a lot of clout.'

Speaking on radio earlier in the day, Newman had let fly. 'I love women. Been married to two or three of them … [But] tell me what they've ever done in football or for football … I'm talking about the people on football clubs. I'm talking about women in football who use football as a vehicle to do whatever else they wish to do that's got nothing to do with football … they have an agenda.'

He continued, 'The AFL does not need shrieking, hysterical, desperate women trying to bob up with causes that they just get their excitement out of, or some self-fulfilling gratification out of, very minor and trivial issues.'

The Western Bulldogs director Dr Susan Alberti, one of the signatories to the Wilson letter, told the *Age* that there was no hidden agenda: 'I thought long and hard about putting my name to this … my only agenda is to make sure women are given the respect they deserve.'

Newman and his co-host Garry Lyon then hit back at Alberti, with Newman implying she was a hypocrite because she had bought front-row tables to a *Footy Show* filming after Newman's controversial stunt (the purchase was later revealed to be part of a donation to a charity fundraiser). The female directors were branded 'liars and hypocrites' because they had included Collingwood's first female board member, Sally Capp, as a signatory to the letter, with Lyon claiming she did not want to be part of it.

Alberti, a prominent businesswoman who had been involved in football for over fifty years, decided to sue both Channel 9 and the two TV personalities for defamation. Eighteen months later, she was awarded a $220,000 settlement from the network. Both Newman and Lyon refused to participate in Channel 9's apology to Dr Alberti, who is now vice-president of the Bulldogs. Outside the Supreme Court, Sam Newman sarcastically joked that he was going to spend his entire summer thinking long and hard about speaking 'carefully.'

*

It is largely believed that the days of hush money are behind football – and with the increasing number of women at board level, this could well be true. Yet cultures of complicity persist. Even for fans in the stands, supporting the game is not as straightforward as it once might have seemed. The notion of looking after 'your' team has been increasingly warped. Instead of going towards the game, club members' money and taxpayer subsidies may end up paying for court trials, settlements, even private detectives to interview witnesses and follow an alleged rape victim in order to build up a dossier. And this complicity, it seems, is not contained; rather, it can seep into other worlds. Over the past ten years, a number of disturbing revelations have emerged alleging special treatment of footballers by police.

# CHAPTER 16

'She's just one of these footy sluts that runs around looking for footballers to fuck,' an officer allegedly said to Senior Detective Scott Gladman, before urging him to drop the case against St Kilda's Stephen Milne.

Six years later, in 2010, the Milne case (in which his teammate Leigh Montagna was also implicated) resurfaced despite the two players being cleared. The detective and sergeant leading the investigation had since left the force and decided to break their silence about the case to Channel 9.

Gladman said other police had seriously hindered the investigation and that the alleged victim's statement was leaked to the club. Unauthorised photocopies of transcripts were made, a missing page being found on a police copier. Recordings of the players' interviews vanished from Gladman's desk for up to seven hours.

'We were told that if things went well, consider yourself a Saints person for life,' Gladman told Channel 9. The former cop's claims were supported by another Victoria Police officer, Mike Smith, who had also worked on the case in 2004. The allegations triggered an Office of Police Integrity investigation. 'They wanted to be seen to be more important in their eyes to the club,' Smith said of some local police. 'Anything they could do to help the club they would do.'

Then, in July 2010, a freedom of information request filed by Australian Associated Press came through. The document was largely blacked out, but the gist was clear: it was a memorandum of understanding struck between Victoria Police and the AFL, a contract which formalised the sharing of files, photos, videos and evidence on people involved in the AFL. The police were required to let the AFL know of any investigations into the league's players and staff, and would contact it before making any public comment. The formality of this intimacy between police and football looked plain ugly to outsiders. It was one thing to hear about individual police officers undermining investigations, but an official document such as this reeked of conspiracy.

*

A similar type of 'football adulation' was discovered after an allegation of rape was reported to police in New South Wales in November 2004. This time, the woman involved was obviously not 'looking for a footy player to fuck' – a tourist from Finland, she could only identify one of the three men involved as the 'surfer guy.' It was the police who recognised Bryan Fletcher, then the captain of the South Sydney rugby league team, sitting alongside the 'surfer guy' in a photo the woman had taken with her disposable camera of the men she had met at a bar before returning home with them. Her night, she reported, slanted sideways, suddenly menacing, when she started having sex with the 'surfer guy' and the others entered the bedroom. She told police she tried to get up, but the surfer guy hadn't finished. He held her down, she said, slapped her and raped her while another guy stuck his dick in her mouth. Much later, when it was light outside and the house was quiet, she crept out of the bed, finding her clothes and handbag – but not her red shoes. Barefoot, she tiptoed past one of the guys, out cold and snoring on the couch. Once on the street, she said, she started running. It was Bondi, she told police, describing the house to them. The police executed two search warrants that day – the first house was the wrong one, but inside the second they found her red shoes.

The woman was taken to the hospital to give samples for a sexual assault kit and a team was put together to investigate the complaint. In February 2005 the case was suspended when police decided there was not enough evidence, while the complainant, having returned to Finland, was reluctant to pursue the charges. The case, however, was revisited three years later when a NSW Police Integrity Commission inquiry unveiled Operation Mallard, an investigation into the alleged cover-up of sexual assault allegations involving Bryan Fletcher.

At the time of the Finnish tourist's allegations, Superintendent Adam 'Gus' Purcell was acting commander of the area in charge of the investigation. Although not part of the actual team investigating her claims, Purcell soon inserted himself into the proceedings once Fletcher was recognised in the photograph.

The inquiry discovered that when Purcell became aware the investigating officers were planning to go around to Fletcher's house, he told them not to. 'He's just been married,' he said.

'She hasn't fingered him yet.' Then Purcell rang Ricky Stuart, who had recently been announced as coach of the 2005 NSW State of Origin team and then of the Sydney Roosters – Fletcher's former team. To the commission Purcell claimed he wanted Fletcher's contact details but didn't feel 'comfortable speaking about it over the phone,' so organised to meet the revered coach in Rushcutters Bay.

According to Purcell, the meeting was brief and cursory. He asked for Fletcher's mobile phone number and told Stuart he could not tell him what it was about. Stuart recalled the meeting differently. Interviewed by the commission, Stuart said Purcell mentioned that:

> Bryan could be in some trouble … It was basically, like, a girl had reported that she had been raped. That she was with a couple of blokes from Bondi in a cab going home and she was drunk and/or, you know, forgotten what the circumstances were, what happened, and there's, you know, every opportunity that Bryan could have been involved and … Could have been involved as in being he was there. Did, did actually … mention to me that they had some photos … and Bryan was in the cab and that they, they picked his picture out, which was the reason why he wanted to come to me, to talk to Bryan.

After meeting with Purcell, the coach rang Fletcher. The captain was pre-warned. Then Purcell called him and arranged a private meeting at Bondi police station in the superintendent's office. It was not recorded. In a later bugged conversation with a colleague, Purcell said he had told Fletcher about the photograph – vital information that could have been used by the investigating police to catch Fletcher out if he tried to provide a false alibi. In the same bugged conversation, Purcell described how he had arranged the meeting:

> Now I went to school with Bryan's brother but there was about fucking thirty years' difference. Dave and I were good mates. That was it. We haven't kept in contact since. So I said, 'Mate, I'm a good mate of Dave's. Can you come in and see me? I'm the Commander of, of … Eastern Suburbs.'

In the weeks and months following the complaint, the superintendent's phone records show that Fletcher made over twenty-five calls to Purcell. When queried about a text message sent at 1 a.m., he said, 'It may have been a congratulations after he had a win.' Purcell even spoke to Fletcher's wife after the captain asked him to reassure her that Fletcher had nothing to do with the rape allegations, and discussed the status of the police investigation with South Sydney's CEO. Less than three months after their first meeting, Fletcher gave Purcell free tickets to a rugby game.

\*

On reading the transcripts of the Operation Mallard report, it's not hard to detect the obvious adrenaline and kick Purcell got out of getting close to, and being needed by, some of rugby league's most influential figures. An amateur rugby player himself, Purcell also coached several teams in the police league. Now here he was, talking to – no, *advising* – professional players on the phone. He was receiving text messages from an A-league player, not to mention his personal meeting with a famous coach.

Then, four months after the assault allegations, less than a month after the case was dropped, Purcell was appointed assistant manager to the Blues, the NSW State of Origin team. His role was to 'help change the culture of rugby league' due to the league's plague of scandals and sexual assault allegations.

Ultimately, the Police Integrity Commission found Purcell 'unfit' to remain a police officer and, as it wound up its report, it included the transcript of a bugged conversation he had in 2006. He had phoned Sergeant Alison Brazel, a colleague who had worked on the case, to tell her the 'goss.'

> PURCELL: I'll tell you this for free. I've heard, ah, now it jogs
>    the memory. When I was down in Melbourne last year for
>    the last Origin game.
>
> BRAZEL: Yeah, yeah.
>
> PURCELL: I, ah, met, who was the guy that you did the
>    search warrant on, who was the main protagonist?
>
> BRAZEL: ———
>
> PURCELL: So I went to a couple of functions and ———'s
>    there. Anyway he came up to me and said, you don't
>    remember me. I said, I don't have a clue who you are. He
>    said I'm, ah ——— or whatever his name is, you're
>    Adam Purcell, thank you very much. I said, mate, no
>    need to thank me, we didn't do any–, I didn't do anything
>    to help ya. And I, I saw him at a couple of other things
>    later on and I said, ah, fuck it, I had a few beers in me

one night. I said, mate, what did happen that night, will
you tell me?

BRAZEL: *[Laughs]* Yeah.

PURCELL: And Bryan Fletcher got a head job on the front,
ah, the front garden.

BRAZEL: Yeah, yeah.

PURCELL: Um, and came in.

BRAZEL: Yeah.

PURCELL: They both started having sex with her and –

BRAZEL: They, Bryan Fletcher?

PURCELL: No … No. The brother, the brother and –––––––.

BRAZEL: Right, right.

PURCELL: And Bryan was watching –

BRAZEL: Right.

PURCELL: – 'cause he'd already got the head job.

BRAZEL: Yeah.

PURCELL: And then she said no, no, that's it –

BRAZEL: Yeah.

PURCELL: – and he ran away.

BRAZEL: He ran away? Bryan Fletcher ran away?

PURCELL: Ran away, ran home.

BRAZEL: *[Laughs]* Right.

PURCELL: And he, he swears that when she said no, that was it.

BRAZEL: And they all stopped.

PURCELL: Yeah. Well, so he said, told me, I don't give a fuck.

BRAZEL: Mmm, mmm.

Purcell sounds pumped. He was, after all, in the thick of it, with
'the boys.'

\*

It is impossible to know how many police officers trying to do their jobs investigating complaints against footballers have been thwarted by this pervading 'the boys are alright' attitude. As for how useful Purcell was in his 'educational' role at the Blues, one can't help but wonder if he taught them about their responsibilities, or just their rights.

Where does this sense of entitlement start? I remember something a footballer told me when he briefly tried out as a rookie in an AFL team. It was the smallest thing, but perhaps this is where the lines begin to blur. He told me about how, when he wore his new uniform home, he stopped to grab a burger and chips. To his unease, the shopkeeper wouldn't let him pay. It was nothing really, he told me, six bucks or something, but still it played on his mind. It was as if the old boundaries and rules were disappearing.

# CHAPTER 17

Next to give evidence was Sarah's friend Olivia Beaumont, her face luminous like a doll's. Nervous, she peered around the courtroom before turning back to Ryan, her big eyes clinging to him. The prosecutor took her through the evening, step by step. It was an airbrushed examination and when Ryan finished, Olivia's eyes widened as defence counsel Thomas stood up to ask his questions.

Thomas asked how long she and Sarah had been friends, and Olivia responded with a high-school certainty – a time when friendship can be easily mapped by grades: 'Year 8, 2003.'

Thomas took her to Eve nightclub. 'Is it fair,' he asked, 'to say that Tom was unhappy that Sarah had gone off with Nate?'

Ryan sprang to his feet. 'I object to the question. What is the relevance of it?'

Taft agreed. 'What is the relevance?'

Thomas shrugged nonchalantly. 'It leads into further text messages,' he responded and added, as if seeing no need to make a fuss, 'I can just take the witness to the text messages.'

That was all Thomas had needed to do, to insinuate that Tom

Shaw liked Sarah a lot more than she liked him – I had been wondering the same thing. But, as Judge Taft queried, what was the relevance?

In terms of real evidence, none whatsoever – but, as Thomas was well aware, seeds of doubt could grow from this insinuation. Why else would Tom be phoning Sarah somewhat manically after she left the club with Nate? And why did she not take any of the calls? Did Sarah feel bad about ignoring his calls? Did guilt add to her distress? With one simple question Thomas had alluded to all of this.

Thomas then asked Olivia about the drive after Eve night-club. She relaxed and said, 'Tom loves driving,' and I saw him, side window open, taking in the night and drunkenly eating McDonald's. Cruising around, the two talked and played music, Tom texting all the while and trying to get through to Sarah.

'Tom was expressing frustration that he couldn't get in touch with Sarah, wasn't he?' said Thomas.

'Yes.'

Again, Ryan objected and again Thomas deferred. Next he brought up the text message Tom sent to Sarah saying they could pick her up.

'You would have gone and picked her up if you had gotten a call from her?' asked Thomas.

'Yes,' said Olivia.

A good friend, I thought, as I watched her wringing her small hands, listening carefully to the questions.

To finish, Thomas asked Olivia about the phone call she had received from Sarah around 11 a.m. the next day.

'The first thing she told you was that she had a $40 cab ride home?' said Thomas.

'Yes.'

Nice, I thought, glancing over at Justin. How very kind of you.

\*

It's not during the act, it's the way you treat them after it. Most of them could have been avoided if they had've put them in a cab and said, you know, thanks for that, sort of thing, not just kicked her out, call her a dirty whatever, that sort of thing. It's how you treat them afterwards that can cover a lot of that sort of stuff up.

When 'Code of Silence' aired footage of a young Newcastle Knights player saying this during an NRL education session, he was howled down in the aftermath. The outrage was anticipated by the program's reporter, Sarah Ferguson, who drily noted, 'The NRL says it is making progress but judging by the final answer from this young player on recent scandals involving group sex, they still have a long way to go.'

For many, this comment epitomised the issue, illustrating that rugby players are a bunch of buffoons who think that being nice to a woman after raping her will head off any problems. And indeed this is a defence that has been put forward in well-publicised cases to explain rape allegations. During the trial of the world champion boxer Mike Tyson, his lawyer contended that the complainant took action not because she was raped, but because Tyson said she could either walk home or take a limousine immediately after sex. The lawyer, Alan Dershowitz, continued:

> This woman came on as a groupie. Everybody knows what the rules are for groupies who hang around famous athletes and rock stars. They get 15 or 20 minutes of not very good sex, no kiss goodnight, no telephone number, no appreciation. All they get are bragging rights – 'I slept with the champ.'

But is this what the inarticulate twenty-year-old rugby player was trying to say – that you could cover up a rape with a few nice words and a taxi fare home? His club didn't think so.

The Knights' chief executive, Steve Burraston, said in the player's defence: 'I understand he was responding to something that they had actually been taught in the training module, and it was along the lines of: if you've gone back and had a relationship with a girl, don't throw her out there; make sure that she gets home; treat her with respect; if you're drunk, don't drive, put her in a taxi and make sure she gets home.'

Justin had said he wanted to make sure Sarah got a taxi home. So does he get a gold star on his Respect & Responsibility test? Hardly. Sure, he offered to walk her to Clarendon Street, but was this so-called gentlemanly act simply a strategy to get laid? Did he see what was on offer in the house and want a piece of the action: first in the alley, and second by 'sharing a cab' and directing it to his place – on the opposite side of town to Sarah's – where she then, sticking to her word that she wanted to go home, found herself paying for an extra ten kilometres?

It could be said that a fair amount of strategising goes into most sexual encounters, but Justin's doggedness makes me uneasy. His asking to be finished off, his decision to have the cab drive to his home first, and then getting Sarah to promise to come over the next afternoon – there was something rotten about this persistence. By his own account it was clear Sarah had had enough. But he wouldn't respect that. He kept pressing. He stayed close.

And why did he say to her, after they left the alleyway, 'You're not going to tell the police Collingwood raped you, are you?' Just how 'off-the-cuff' was that? Did he say it because she was upset – and if so, why was she upset? And if she was upset and had obviously had enough, why did he persist in trying to get her to go home with him? Did he think she was a spittoon for one boy after another to come in? After all, he hadn't managed to finish the job with her in the alley – did he now want another chance?

Why didn't he see her as fully human?

And yet – again by his own account – Justin was better behaved than the other young men in the house that night. After having their way with her, none showed any inclination to see her home (seeing her to the front door seemed hard enough), let alone phoned the next day to check if she was okay. But then again, would Justin have offered to see her home if he'd managed to have sex with her in the house alongside the others?

Justin wasn't thinking of Sarah so much as he was thinking of how to leverage off his mates, how to get in on the act. He was thinking about scoring. He was hardly a gentleman. But by whose standards should we judge him?

Burraston said of the Knights player, 'He didn't articulate it very well, and that's the danger.' By 'danger,' did the CEO mean that all of us – players, critics, support staff, fans, spokespeople, academics, feminists, the media – keep getting confused over what we're talking about?

Is it rape, or is it treating women like shit? Speaking to the *Sydney Morning Herald*, an anonymous NRL player had said that, 'Players get a lot of attention from girls in the clubs because they've got a high profile. That's not the players' fault. Most of the time the girl goes back willingly and consents to everything, but sometimes regrets it when she wakes up in the morning and says, "I didn't want that to happen," and that's when the problems start. I don't know one single guy in the NRL who would resort to holding a woman down against her will or raping her, and nobody would condone that. I do see what they're saying about risk; you just never know how a girl's going to react afterwards. You're not supposed to say it publicly, but everyone knows that if you're polite afterwards and pay her cab fare home you usually don't have any problems.'

Could that be true? That jumping on the Xbox after consensually gangbanging a girl, or high-fiving others in the room and letting the woman make her own way out, could motivate her to make a rape allegation?

If young men are going to be educated about rape and consent, as the AFL and NRL are trying to do, then they need to be taught about respect and decent behaviour as well – before, during and after sex – and not have their adolescent attempts to struggle through the nuances of relationships subjected to jibes from those who think everything about sex is obvious.

*

In 2004, Dr Angela Williams helped to develop the program about respect for women within AFL football clubs – and spent two years in the league's clubrooms, talking to players about her work and their relationships with women.

'It was momentous when Andrew Demetriou publicly asked all women who felt they'd been assaulted by a football player to come forward,' she recalled, adding that the AFL was one of the first organisations in Australia to have a program for men about the abuse of women. 'Traditionally we've always spoken to women.'

In hindsight this seemed obvious, but it still came as a revelation to me. I thought about all the sexual assault awareness education fed to schools – it was as if only half of the job was being done. How to avoid being raped, not how to avoid being a rapist. Except that many complaints to police and calls to rape crisis centres revealed something different – girls are being raped at parties, on dates, by men they meet on a nightclub dance floor, by their peers. And when these perpetrators are called to account, their jaw drops. They're not guilty, most say.

To be guilty, do you have to have some idea of doing something wrong? And here we may be starting from a long way back. During the same NRL education session for the Newcastle Knights, the educators attempted to reveal to the players how a sexual act they might consider to be consensual could well be rape.

A DVD showed a drunk woman going home with two men, drinking with them in the kitchen, all three having a great time (during our conversation Williams made the point that while a woman may be thinking 'safety in numbers' going back to a house with a guy and his mates, the men may be thinking, 'Oh, we're all going to get a go').

The woman in the video agrees to have sex with one of them, who then ducks out of the bedroom, pulling up his trousers and gesturing to his mate to take over. The camera cuts to the woman coming out of the bedroom in a teary rage, pulling her clothes back on, yelling at the first guy, 'I thought it was you.'

After the film, the group had a discussion. 'She put out first,' said one of the young players, another adding that she had flirted with both of them.

Then a second DVD was shown, revealing a couple of men getting drunk together and getting along. One man helps the other man – now extremely drunk – back to his apartment and has sex with him. In the morning, the victim wakes up, puts on his clothes and rushes out of the apartment, immediately on his phone to a sexual health clinic.

A moaning male angst soundtrack played while the watching players' eyes went moist, their lips parting slightly. When the film finished, the group was silent.

The teacher asked how they thought the man might be feeling.

'Shattered,' said one player.

Another piped up, 'You don't really ask for trouble if you have too much to drink and get raped by a bloke. You don't ask for that.'

'Can we see that there's some sort of double standard that may apply here?' said Mark O'Neill, the former rugby league player running the seminar. It was an interesting tactic – playing on homophobia to convey a point about treating women properly – and yet it was difficult to be sure the young players understood the two-way street they were being taken down. You could see their brows crease as they tried to get their heads around it.

\*

At a panel on pornography at the Sydney Writers' Festival, the writer Kate Holden, a former sex worker, recounted an incident at a brothel she had worked in when two young men, 'somewhere over eighteen and under twenty,' requested to come on her face.

'What we'd really like to do is ejaculate on your face.' Holden recalled them saying. 'I said, "Oh, I don't think so."'

'But wouldn't you like it?' they replied.

'I said, "Well, not a lot, why would you think I would enjoy that?"'

'We've seen lots of porn movies – you know, the money shot.'

'Well, apart from the fact I'd have to redo all my make-up, there are sexual health issues … and it's just not a very nice thing to do.'

In pornography, the women tend to be ecstatic to have men ejaculate on their faces – but they're acting. These two customers, explained Holden, were not yet able to differentiate between life and porn. She went on to say that in the majority of her experiences, both at work and in her everyday life, she found men were more likely to be stupid in bed than malign. 'I think very few people understand how many men are kind of cretinous in bed, but it's out of ignorance rather than spite.'

But this court case is not about ignorance, is it? It's about rape. Surely the two things are not the same? And I guess here is where the complicated clause in a conviction of rape comes in

– was the accused *aware* that the victim was not or might not be consenting or was he indifferent either way? In the bedroom, did the guys believe Sarah was consenting? Did they care? And in the laneway?

# CHAPTER 18

'They want to go where their teammates have been before them,' Charmyne Palavi wrote in the *Daily Telegraph* in 2009 of the rugby players who contacted her for sex, adding that anyone who thought the gangbang culture was going to change 'just because the story's out there … are kidding themselves.'

'Code of Silence' had introduced Palavi to the nation, a forty-year-old Brisbane woman who ran a tanning salon and sought out the company of footballers. The media quickly dubbed her 'the cougar' and a spate of racy tabloid headlines was created in her honour. 'Cougar bags fresh trophies,' read one.

In the *Telegraph*, Palavi continued:

> I was messaging a young player, a Facebook friend, last week and asked what he was doing. He replied: 'Learning how to respect women. LOL (laugh out loud).'
>
> I wrote back: 'Yeah, and I'm still a virgin.'

Critics of footballers' behaviour towards women tend to think of the players as acting out in 'normal' heterosexual scenarios, but the reality is that for many, this is not the case. Footballers may find themselves in a world – and get used to this world – where the 'normal' barriers to consent don't exist.

\*

When the rape allegations against Stephen Milne were raised in 2004, the former AFL footballer and coach Tim Watson wrote an opinion piece in the *Age*:

> Count the number of people you have heard say in the past 24 hours, 'If there was going to be an AFL club involved in a sex scandal it had to be St Kilda.'
>
> An AFL coach told me only hours after the Saints' story broke of a club trip to the country in the past six weeks. Upon arrival the coach spelt it out to the players they were on a training trip and that even though they would be socialising at different stages, alcohol was prohibited.
>
> On the first night in the town, the players and officials were welcomed at a function where the players mingled with the locals. A couple of girls made it clear to everyone that they were keen to attract the attention of a couple of the players. One girl was so convinced of her intentions she sidled up to the coach to explain to him what she planned to do later in the night to one of his players.
>
> The team left the function as a group and went back to the hotel without the adoring fans. At 2am they were woken up by loud banging on doors by the girls from the function. A senior player eventually convinced the girls they were in the wrong place and that they should head home.

Wow, I thought on first reading Watson's piece, that must have been 'scary' for the boys. And I wasn't the only one who reacted badly. 'Some AFL blokes don't know there's a difference between sex and rape,' wrote Phil Cleary, a commentator and former footballer, on *Online Opinion*.

> Seemingly oblivious of the circumstances of the present case, Watson recounted the antics of amorous women in the football subculture. Yet, strangely, none of the examples he offered had anything to do with rape.
>
> With this simple sleight of hand Watson unwittingly reinforced many of the prejudices that beset women who 'cry rape.' Suddenly the alleged perpetrator had become the victim, and it was women who were implicated in, if not blamed for, allegations of rape. After all, how can young footballers avoid an allegation of rape when women are banging at their door at 2am?

Cleary went on to write:

> Tim, this isn't a 'sex scandal.' A sex scandal is Charles having it off with Camilla, or Lady Di with the butler. A woman who alleges sexual assault is claiming to have been the victim of an act of criminal violence.

The timing of Watson's piece was irrefutably bad – but it said, no doubt, what many inside and outside the game were thinking: that a rape allegation could just as easily be reinterpreted as a sex scandal. And that different rules apply to the world of football when it comes to sex.

To a degree, this is true. Tony Wilson recalled being wide-eyed as high-profile players told him about bedding 100 women in a year, keeping tally cards and sharing girls. Wilson said that in no other part of society did he encounter the same sense of competition when it came to women.

'Maybe at high school,' he conceded, 'but the ease of access for these players was ...' Wilson trailed off, wonder still evident on his face. 'In all other interactions in my life, women were the regulating factor. The moderating factor is the handbrake that women put on male sexuality. Perhaps that's a sexist comment, but that's how it appeared to me. At the footy club, however, there was a horde of women that wanted to sleep with footballers, and vice versa. It was, in large part, symbiotic.'

But should the prevalence of groupies and allegations of rape be part of the same conversation? Are groupies complicit in promoting a rape culture? Wilson shrugged and said he didn't know the answers to those questions, but what he did know was that the 'normal consent filters were definitely jeopardised.'

'If Buddy Franklin were sitting here on his own for two hours,' he waved his hand at the empty café seats around us, 'the opportunity to have sex would have arisen, no doubt. But for the rest of us, you need to find an interested partner. And footballers are creatures of habit, they're repetitive, you learn a pattern in the game, an agreed framework, and it's the same with sexual encounters, and these are situations where the normal barriers are not put up by women, and so any exception to *their* norm would be difficult for them to understand, which is where they're getting into trouble. If an encounter is ever not the same, there'll be trouble.'

The words of Mike Tyson's lawyer came back to me. *Everybody knows what the rules are for groupies who hang around famous athletes and rock stars.*

And if you don't know the rules? What about the nineteen-year-old girl in New Zealand whose hotel room just kept filling up with more and more players – was she coached beforehand about these rules? And Sarah?

'I don't know what her problem is,' said an unnamed woman to a reporter after the second Canterbury Bulldogs rape allegations in Coffs Harbour. Having been involved in many a 'club bun,' the woman continued, 'I always had a great time.'

I guess Sarah's 'problem' was that she didn't know the rules.

Writing in the *Guardian* in 2004 under the pseudonym 'Amanda Hughes,' a woman described her experiences as a football groupie in England, catching 'the bug' when she was eighteen years old and feeling the thrill of a player – a man whose name millions were wearing on the backs of their T-shirts – writing down her phone number, a thrill often exceeding five-minute drunken fumbles or one dropping his trousers and saying, 'Suck it.'

'Once you were in a player's room he would encourage you to allow his mates to join in,' wrote Hughes. 'I never understood why – the argument seemed to be that it was "only fair" that they have the same as he was having. I cringe to think of it … But if I'm honest it wasn't the footballer's behaviour that upset me – it was the fact that I was complicit in it, that I said nothing to challenge them. I let the cycle continue.'

There's talk of players now filming gangbang encounters on their mobile phones, not just for a laugh and to show around, but also to prove that 'she,' whatever her name is, was consenting – that she was 'up for it.' Some of these players will point to a smile on the girl's face in their footage, and say, 'See! See!'

\*

During Charmyne Palavi's interview on *Four Corners*' 'Code of Silence,' she described an encounter with a player in which he showed her a video on his phone that he and his teammates had made of getting head from some 'slurry from around Cronulla.' He told her they had videoed it to prove she'd consented.

'And that freaked me out,' said Palavi. 'This girl was actually in her twenties and [he] told me what they did to her. He said they made her put bunny ears on 'cause Easter's coming up and made her give head to all of the players one after the other.'

'Code of Silence' had made a link between groupies and rape, albeit one that was difficult to define.

> SARAH FERGUSON: If some young footballers mistakenly
> think all women want to have sex with them, Charmyne
> Palavi is one who doesn't necessarily discourage the idea.
> She's getting ready for a night on the town with her
> girlfriends, applying the finishing touches, bronzer to
> her legs.

In the interview, Palavi spoke about pursuing footballers for sex and allowing her Facebook page to be used by players and girls to hook up. In practically the same breath, she said that an NRL player had raped her when she drank too much, but the impression given was that this bad experience hadn't put her off. As she talked, a string of text messages popped up on her phone. She showed them to Ferguson, who was taken aback. Viewers got the impression that they were mostly from rugby players, and mostly pictures of their dicks.

In the aftermath of 'Code of Silence' Palavi was hung out to dry. Three days later, the radio host Steve Price discussed the show on air with the reporter Peter Ford. They soon got on to the subject of Palavi.

FORD: ... that lady Charmyne Palavi –
PRICE: Yes.
FORD: – who sets herself up as some kind of matchmaker or
      madam or something. Now she claims that –
PRICE: Can I use another word?
FORD: Yeah.
PRICE: Slut.

Palavi sought damages for defamation from Price and 2UE. But after two years of legal wrangling and a trial which largely consisted of scrutinising Palavi's sexual relationships with footballers, which the defence submitted as proof of the truth of claims that she was a slut, the jury took just twenty minutes to throw out the case, siding – and essentially agreeing – with Price's label.

The jury, as is required, simply reflects the common man and woman.

Not long after 'Code of Silence' aired, Palavi lashed out at her critics and her portrayal on the program. 'If you believed

*Four Corners,*' she wrote, 'I'm supposed to be the NRL's biggest groupie, a wannabe WAG who dresses up, heads out to clubs and hunts down players to have sex with.'

'I'm no angel,' she continued, 'but I've seen this game play out from both sides: First as the partner of a pro footballer for nine years, then as a single woman who can have sex whenever, with whomever, I choose. I am old enough and wise enough to know these encounters are nothing more than what they were at the time – mostly consensual, one-on-one sex, on my terms.'

She went on to describe 'real' groupies, writing that, 'They know where they go out after games, where they stay, when they are in town, with many booking themselves into the same hotels as the teams. I've got one girlfriend in Brisbane who sits down at the beginning of the year with the NRL draw and works out where she's going to follow them (North Queensland Cowboys) for the year.'

Palavi, however, saw herself not as a star-struck groupie, but rather as a woman in control of her sexuality, a woman with agency. So is Palavi an empowered woman, purely interested in the physical and catering to her desires? Does she have power, as Roy Masters suggested, during a 'group sex' encounter with players? 'When the girl is giving them marks for degree of difficulty,' he wrote, 'like dives being scored off the high-board, she is the one with the power in the room.'

Is this the ideal scenario, where the lone female is one of the humiliators, not the humiliated? Or is she simply a 'loophole' woman, as Ariel Levy put it in her book *Female Chauvinist Pigs*: a woman who may 'be the exception that proves the rule, and the rule is that women are inferior'? Has Palavi fallen for a ruse of empowerment, only to find herself complicit in a male subculture that refers to women as 'meat' and 'buns'?

When Sarah Ferguson asked what the appeal of footballers was, Palavi replied, 'They've just got really good bodies.' So, by objectifying players' bodies, has the 'cougar' levelled the playing field? Hardly. In a discussion about the large number of female fans at AFL games on ABC's Radio National fifteen years ago, the feminist historian Dr Margaret Lindley refused to make a comparison between the sexual objectification of women and female fans perving on footballers. 'A footballer is not a stationary object,' said Lindley, 'and not being stationary is actually very important.' She continued:

> A moving object that is powerful, that is surging, and that moreover is moving not for the sake of the observers – none of those players are moving for our sake, for our pleasure, they are doing something for their own, their team's purposes. And to some degree they are completely oblivious of us. They may hear us, but they're not performing for us in some sense ... Now if you take the strip show: a woman or a man in a strip show is a posed object, even when they move. Every move is designed not to express themselves, their energy, their goals, their motives, but simply to – 'I think you will be pleased if I move in this way.'

Women who seek out footballers to fuck aren't equal – and it's not necessarily because of the fucking. It's their level of commitment to the cause, the preening and seeking, that gives it away. They're not the same, they're mirrors for the players to check themselves out in. As Virginia Woolf wrote in 1928,

Women have served all these centuries as looking glasses possessing the magic and delicious power of reflecting the figure of man at twice its natural size.

A footballer does not look at another human when he fucks a groupie. He's looking at his glorified reflection – and when he performs, he's doing it for 'the boys,' not her.

\*

Justin's offering to see Sarah home was opportunistic. There was something rotten, something off, and perhaps something naïve too, about his persistence. Of that much I can be certain. But the rest is murky. Treating women like shit shades into a culture of abuse, which in turn can shade into rape.

# CHAPTER 19

In America, Savannah Dietrich felt betrayed when the court offered what she considered a lenient plea bargain to the two teenagers who had assaulted her. Ignoring a gag order, she went public – a stance that saw the defendants' lawyers file a contempt of court charge, which they quickly withdrew as the public raged in support of her. The court was also caught unawares by the attention and the plea bargain was altered, albeit minutely. But it was enough for Dietrich: the public support she found via social media and the judicial process (not the result) saw her emerge from her experience with an unexpected power. Of her case, Amanda Hess wrote in the online magazine *Slate*:

> the criminal justice process can also rob the victim of control over her own narrative. Reporting to official channels often means keeping quiet in social ones. But here, Dietrich is the editor of her own story. She has the power to delete the comments she doesn't like and promote the ones she does. Thanks to a few brave tweets, a 17-year-old rape victim is

now curating an international conversation about sexual assault in America.

Sound familiar?

Kimberley Duthie is an Australian teenager whose name, by law, no one ought to have known. And while the differences between Dietrich and Duthie are stark – the American teenager was astoundingly clear about her motives in going public, refused all offers of finance and was supported by her family, while Duthie was confused and naïve, her motives murky – both sought to regain their power and voice through the social media, challenging the channels that stifled them.

The fuse was lit in May 2010 with claims that a sixteen-year-old had slept with two St Kilda footballers who visited her school, had a relationship with a 23-year-old player, Sam Gilbert, and was now pregnant. When she confided in her school principal, the principal immediately reported her claim to the Education Department and the police. It didn't take long for the news to get around. And while investigating police later asserted that contact had come after the school visit and no charges would be laid, it was too late. Word had spread far beyond St Kilda Football Club, through the AFL, the Victorian police force and, finally, to the media.

Then, just days before Christmas, after newspapers refused to publish – the *Herald Sun* said they'd offered her counselling instead – the teenager posted online the photographs of three St Kilda footballers, dubbed 'Dickileaks.'

The captain, Nick Riewoldt, is naked and shrugging comically as a younger player, Zac Dawson, holds a condom wrapper close to his penis. It looks like a photo with a 'before' story, but at a press conference Riewoldt solemnly assured the public that he had just woken up and was snapped as he got out of bed. In the second photo, mid-fielder Nick Dal Santo is lying on a bed, holding his penis as if in preparation for a wank. And although the teenager claimed she had taken them, it was said – and later confirmed – that the players took these photos of each other while on a footy trip in Miami.

The lawyer Ross Levin, St Kilda's club vice-president, threatened to tie the teenager up in litigation for the next fifteen years of her life. A Federal Court ruling appeared to resolve the matter, with the judge ordering the photos be removed, no others posted, and requiring the young woman and the club to undertake mediation.

Few observers acknowledged the eerie familiarity of the teenager's choice of font for her Christmas e-card. Over the images she had typed in red italic font, *Merry Christmas, Courtesy of the St Kilda School Girl!* Duthie was referencing a viral email that had circulated after her principal went to the police, an email which made its way through the AFL Players Association, to present and past footballers, footy staff, online forums, various government departments, law firms and police officers.

Attached to the viral email was a photo of Duthie taken from her Facebook page. She was wearing black leggings and a St Kilda jersey cut off at the midriff. Someone had typed 'The Saints Girl' (in the same font Duthie used for her counterstrike) over the top. Also circulating was a digitally altered movie poster for *Three Men and a Baby*, with the actors' heads replaced with those of the players believed to have slept with her.

The internet suddenly became Duthie's schoolyard. 'I just wanted you guys to feel how I felt,' she later said of the photos.

'I was not sleeping for days on end,' she told the journalist Peter Munro. 'I would just sit up on my laptop reading article after article about myself. I was just so obsessed with wanting to know what the world was saying about me and trying to defend myself at the same time.'

When she posted the photos, Duthie was holidaying with her parents in a Gold Coast motel room. By the time her parents settled in front of the television for the night, their daughter was on the evening news, bizarrely in a room that looked exactly like the room they were in. Scores of Australians watched as Duthie spoke to her laptop, manically tossing her long brown hair and answering her mobile phone to torrents of abuse.

'Okay,' she said feverishly, leaning into the video camera on her computer, 'so everyone wants to know what I'm fucking really feeling like. I can't even explain it. Do you know how fucking angry I am with everyone? Oh my god, I could fucking SCREAM.'

When Duthie flew into Melbourne airport, a media scrum was waiting. It was the same year that Kerri-Anne Kennerley warned footballers that they 'put themselves in harm's way by picking up strays.' As Duthie approached the waiting media – dressed in shiny black heels, a black blazer over a short dress, a tattoo on the inside of her wrist like an entry stamp into a nightclub – it was as if the 'stray' had been conjured. Her parents – the teenager told reporters – had taken the bus home and she was not welcome to join them. The media hung on her every word, dutifully blurring her face, which just brought her young body in its skimpy clothing to the fore.

*

The teenager's Twitter feed grew to over 20,000 followers. Her blog, *The Small Girl, With a Big Voice*, became an online 'go-to.' On radio, men fought over whether she was a child or not, and whether it was illegal to sleep with her.

'This kid is seventeen, and she's talking about drugs, alcohol and sex,' said a holier-than-thou Neil Mitchell.

Each time the AFL urged the media not to feed on the teenager, the governing football body was accused of trying to sweep her under the carpet. The *Herald Sun* ran a story headlined 'Tortured Teen in a Bloke's World' accompanied by a photo of Duthie, her back to the camera, leaning against a graffitied wall.

'Jane, now 17, is articulate, intelligent and beautiful. She is tough, but to adults she likes, polite,' read the text beneath the photo.

Proclaiming to be speaking on behalf of all women mistreated by footballers, Duthie attended St Kilda's first training session and threw flimsy placards on the ground that read 'St Scandal,' 'HU$H,' 'AFL (All Fucking Lies.)' and 'Respect: Can you spell that for me AFL?' Female columnists wrote about her 'chutzpah,' while older journalists reported wide-eyed on her ability to text, tweet, film and take photos on her assortment of mobile phones.

Journalists just couldn't help it. They were addicted to her, and she to them. On his blog, the broadcaster Derryn Hinch related for his readers a meeting he had had with Ricky Nixon, the manager of the footballers caught up in the drama. Nixon had 'repeatedly, and piously, expressed his concerns for the girl's wellbeing' before handing Hinch an editorial he had drafted for him to read out on 3AW, imploring the media to cease covering the story in the interests of Duthie's welfare. It had even been signed off with 'I'm Derryn Hinch,' the renowned radio host's signature tagline. But it was how Nixon wound up the meeting that Hinch says shocked him. 'Any man would want to eff her,' Nixon said.

'About ten days later, she says he did,' wrote Hinch.

\*

For all the new measures the AFL had put in place – its Respect & Responsibility policy and protocols for players and clubs – the league hadn't factored in a sixteen-year-old being ridiculed by a bunch of well-paid young men, their older colleagues, support staff and fans, let alone her childish revenge.

They most certainly hadn't factored in the 'honey trap' the teenager set, with the help of a *Herald Sun* journalist, for Ricky Nixon. In the months before, Nixon had made a complaint about Duthie to police, saying she had turned up at his office with a water bottle filled with vodka, demanding money for the Riewoldt photos (Nixon was his manager), and that she had tried to strip in his office. Nixon said he took photos of her on his mobile phone to protect himself. Obviously treasuring the photos well beyond his police complaint, Nixon had shown these photos to Derryn Hinch.

A week later, Duthie released footage of Nixon's alleged coke-snorting habits and their affair – Nixon himself appearing in his undies in her hotel room, accommodation paid for by St Kilda Football Club – to the media. She was applauded. 'You're amazing,' gushed radio host Kate Langbroek. 'We salute you.' Miranda Devine, now at the *Daily Telegraph*, called her 'an Avenging Angel.' Meanwhile, Nixon, protesting his innocence, in a voice quivering with self-pity, said on radio, 'This is the thanks I get,' claiming he had been helping Duthie with her 'life plan' after talking to her parents to offer his help in counselling her.

He did eventually admit to visiting the teenager at her hotel room on at least three occasions – including Valentine's Day – although he denied they had sex. It was football at its trashiest, and it dirtied everyone – from players, to agents, to coaches, to league head honchos – Nixon was, after all, a friend of the AFL's chief executive, Andrew Demetriou – to fans and, finally, to the media, which had built the game up to be larger than life, only to drag it down. And so when, amid the headiness of the Nixon saga, Duthie appeared on *60 Minutes* (the Channel 9 show is believed to have paid her a five-figure sum) and told the reporter Liz Hayes that she had never been pregnant, it was as if a spell had been lifted and everyone was naked, muddied and a little bit ashamed.

'I don't know why I did it,' she said. 'I was a stupid immature little teenager.' The convincing photos she had put on the internet of her holding her pregnant belly were fake. In one photo Duthie's eyes are wide and she has her hand over her mouth in mock-horror. She is wearing a bra and St Kilda footy shorts. Oops, her expression says, look who got me pregnant! It now appears that she made herself look pregnant by sucking air into her very elastic abdomen.

To make matters worse, Andrew Demetriou subtly chastised journalists when he revealed on air that he had been aware that something wasn't quite right about the girl's claim. 'I was led to believe through some of our other investigations that that may have been the case [she was not pregnant] but as you know … there has been a number of occasions whereby this young girl has said things that have proven to be incorrect and that's why we've chosen all along … to act responsibly and not play this out through the media,' he told 3AW. The media lapsed into an uneasy silence, and the clamour to write the definitive piece on the St Kilda Schoolgirl was over.

*

Kimberley Duthie was never going to be a heroine for women's rights, for taking on the big boys at the AFL. In fact, she turned out to be the opposite, reinforcing the archaic stereotype of a lying female. But what was interesting was how much the public wanted her to be. And in this sense, Duthie became the weapon for other people's misgivings about football.

'This is not a story about Ricky Nixon per se,' Andrew Demetriou said at a press conference. 'This is a story about a girl – a child – and we are concerned about her welfare.'

When asked if Nixon's behaviour had tarnished the league, Demetriou shook his head. 'I repeat, Ricky Nixon doesn't speak for the AFL,' he said. 'The AFL is an organisation that everyone knows, full well, knows through me, on numerous occasions what our view is on our Respect & Responsibility program and how we dearly, dearly, treasure shifting the attitude of people towards women in our industry.'

And indeed the league itself had tried its hardest with Duthie, offering her and her family support as well as being in contact with the Education Department, the Department of Human Services, welfare support services and Victoria Police about her welfare. But the problem was that while the AFL may well have done the right thing by Duthie, it was too late. The St Kilda players, their club and their manager had already done the damage.

At the very inception of her pregnancy lie, a manipulative ploy turned placebo test for the boys, Duthie said Sam Gilbert stopped returning her calls. The team's skipper told her to 'Fuck off, you slag' and another player sent her a text message urging her to kill herself. The club's management had brought her in and coached her on what to say to police investigating whether the players had acted inappropriately at her school. After she released the photos, the club threatened a lawsuit, while Ricky Nixon extended the bullying arm, making threatening remarks to Duthie's school principal and showing the photos of the semi-undressed Duthie in his office to anyone who'd look.

Nixon, before checking himself into rehab, continued to deny having an affair with the teenager, saying only that he'd had 'inappropriate dealings' with her. He told the *Australian* that he was 'struggling with the shock of being set up. I feel sick how it's all being discussed, but I'll try to hang in.'

The AFL Players Association, responsible for accrediting managers, ran an investigation into Nixon, headed up by none other than David Galbally, while Nixon's agency teetered on collapse as players began a mass exodus. The association's report, which was leaked to the press, quoted Nick Riewoldt saying he would like to 'punch his lights out' if the accounts of his manager's relationship with Duthie proved to be true.

Nixon's accreditation was suspended for two years and his marriage ended. In March 2013 he was found guilty of charges unrelated to the Duthie episode, including holding his (now ex-) fiancé against her will, threatening her with a kitchen knife and resisting arrest.

*

What Kimberley Duthie now aspires to is a mystery. When she was fifteen, she was the youngest mountain runner selected to represent Australia in Italy and became the Under 18 national champion. An interstate competitor for hurdles, long jump, high jump and running, she was a naïve schoolgirl who ate, trained, studied and slept. Then suddenly she was living in hotels paid for by St Kilda Football Club as part of a deal struck on the condition that she make a public apology and delete the photos she posted on the internet. She was also to issue a statement that the players involved with her met her socially after a match and not at her school.

In eighteen months, she had tested and stretched the plastic tape of child protection around her, like a hatchling just out of its shell – and predators were quick to detect her nubile vulnerability.

A 34-year-old police constable who arrested the teenager for shoplifting was suspended and charged with twelve offences, including sexual penetration of a seventeen-year-old under his care. The prosecution claimed the constable rang the girl's father and said he would introduce her to programs for troubled teens. Ricky Nixon, too, had offered to 'help' her.

And yet, Kimberley Duthie had caught football's dark side off-guard.

This is what the club repeatedly failed to understand in its dealings with her. She was a top athlete when she first met the St Kilda players, and while she was flattered by their attentions, she wanted more than to be their sexual plaything. Duthie wanted to be one of them. When she was cut off from the team, this highly competitive teenager had her first inkling of the limitations of her sex – and so she broke the rule that bonds all football players. What happens on the footy trip stays on the footy trip.

# CHAPTER 20

I bought a watery hot chocolate from the red-brick cafeteria and wandered down the steps onto the Box Hill oval where people, mostly women and girls rugged up in beanies and coats, were mucking around, kicking footballs to one another while two teams were warming up near the goal posts. The teams had jogged out of the change rooms and through a line of cheering supporters before dissolving into lunges and squats.

It was the Victorian Women's Football League's grand final and the ground was filling up with spectators. It had taken me half an hour to find a park for my car, all the while stopping for groups of girls as they crossed the highway. I'd caught the tail end of the reserves' grand final and winced as the two teams scrambled clumsily for the ball. Their kicks were messy and the tackles slow. I wondered if I should avoid writing about women's footy if it turned out not to be that great. The siren sounded.

I watched as volunteers in the box behind the scoreboard manually removed the numbers and replaced them with zeroes. It was time for the top teams in the premier league, the Darebin Falcons and Diamond Creek, to clash. I drained the dregs of my drink in its Styrofoam cup as the players faced off, the ball held aloft in the centre square by the umpire. On the bounce the girls sprang forward, fingers outstretched.

They were good. Long-limbed and athletic, when they stormed past the railing, the sound was like a thunder of hooves at the races. The tackles were fast, players hitting the ground with a thwack as the crowd flinched and then roared with approval. And the kicks – the odd tongue poking out of the side of the mouth in concentration, a neat drop on the foot – were clean.

\*

'When we played our first game, the senior male football players at the club made a real day of it,' said Debbie Lee, president of the Victorian Women's Football League. 'They hired a portable spa and set it up at the railings where they drank and laughed at us.' It was 1991 and Lee had started up a female football team in Sunshine, in Melbourne's west. She was nineteen. 'People thought that I wanted to prove something, that I wanted to beat men, but I loved footy. I wanted to play.'

Lee wasn't the only woman who wanted to play Aussie Rules, or the first. She showed me a photograph from 1918 of a female football team, wearing striped jumpers and caps, baggy shorts, long socks and leather boots, their arms folded. 'There is actually a history of women's footy,' she said – and I suddenly thought about all those female spectators in their long dresses and umbrellas secretly yearning to run onto the oval, to throw their bodies around freely and take a mark. Indeed, Nikki Wedgwood at the University of Sydney discovered a quote in a magazine published in 1876 by a Melbourne private school, where one girl was 'bold enough to suggest' that a football club be formed for girls because she saw how much 'fun, enjoyment and excitement' the boys got out of the game.

But for the most part, these early games of footy were a piss-take. Males wore dresses to umpire while footage of a fund-raising game between the Newport Aircraft Girls and the Railway Girls during World War II was accompanied by comments such as 'Goody goody!', 'Oh, Grace forgot her lipstick!' and, lastly, 'This game is to prove that a women's place is in the home.'

Even so, girls and women persisted.

In 2003, three schoolgirls took Football Victoria to court for the right to keep playing football as they had reached the cut-off age for females to compete in their local competition. Their action forced the hand of the league, which then set up a competition for female teenagers. Participation has grown across the league from 20,000 females in 2005 to almost 95,000 in 2012. The AFL's tagline is: 'You kick like a girl. Good for you!'

But of course, to many in the game, females playing footy is a joke. In the early nineties, Debbie Lee and a few other female players were invited on *The Footy Show*. Naïvely, they accepted. 'But the panellists just wanted to take the piss,' recalled Lee. 'They asked about our breasts and about the "blood rule." I just had to play along.'

\*

'Do you think the standard of female footy could reach that of men's, at least at a VFL level?'

'No.'

'Not even in fifty years?'

'No.'

'One hundred years?'

'No.'

Ian Aitken shook his head at me. He was amused. 'What does it matter?' he asked. 'I'm not being sexist, it's the reality of it, but that's not to take away from the fact that participation is growing.' A former VFL football player, he was most famous for playing in the 'Battle of Britain,' a showcase Aussie Rules game in England in 1987 that turned into a bloodbath. ('The spectators thought it was hilarious,' he recalled. 'At half-time, they were allowed on the oval to have a go and they just jumped on whoever had the ball and punched them. That's how they figured the game was played.') Now Aitken coaches footy teams, among them both an Under 16 and Under 12 girls.

I tried one more time. 'Are you sure? I mean, it's not just about a single generation of females, is it?' Aitken looked even more bemused, but I kept going. 'We've only been truly free to play sport, to be physical, for about fifty years, so females have got a lot of catching up in terms of strength and muscle to do, don't you think? We probably haven't even reached our potential yet.'

I described a series of photos I'd seen showing how girls started out throwing a ball just like boys, but over time they started to use less space and shrink their movement, while the boys continued to use their entire bodies and take up all the space they needed. Sure, there were biological differences between us, I said, but many were also cultural.

Aitken shook his head. 'What does it matter?' he asked again. 'The girls are having fun, who cares if they'll ever be as good as the guys?'

I slumped. He was right – they're having fun, what does anything else matter? And I knew it was unrealistic to contemplate women playing football at AFL level in the near future, but I kept thinking about the Nicky Winmar moment – that defiant and proud act of pulling up his football jersey and pointing to his black skin. His presence, his agency – it was purely physical and yet he demanded respect. Could there ever be a Winmar moment for females in football?

'It's an intoxicating feeling,' Tony Wilson had said to me. 'To execute a play, to control the ball and your opponent. It's a feeling that will not be repeated in any other area of my life. Everything else is nuanced, but football was simple and it was something I did really well.'

I felt a surge of anger when he said this, and said, somewhat stupidly, 'We get that feeling too.' He looked confused. 'Women do,' I said. 'Women get that feeling too when they play sport. That sixth sense of knowing where everything is.'

\*

Both football leagues, the AFL and NRL, are trying to change their cultures, to instil a respect for women in their players and the broader community – but can they? Is it possible for women to have a Nicky Winmar moment in football if they remain on the sidelines? Surely this is an issue much bigger than football, an issue that saw the Australian women's basketball team flying to the 2012 London Olympics in economy while the men's team flew business class (it had been hoped that 2012 would be the first Games in which women athletes would be fielded by all participating countries, but such hopes were dashed).

But even if women's sport is often trivialised, is the liberating power of playing sport really diminished? Would getting equal pay, equal crowds, equal media coverage make the world a better place?

And what if the likes of Kimberley Duthie were respected by footballers for their athleticism? Would they change jock culture, or become a part of it?

And a final question, one that perhaps underlies all of this – if women get stronger, do men get weaker? In *Women and Sports*, the American writer Janice Kaplan wrote about the 1978 cliff-diving championships, a competition held annually in Mexico. That year, however, a Texan woman had qualified for the finals and the male participants threatened to withdraw if she did not. She was subsequently disqualified.

One of the Mexican competitors explained: 'This is a death-defying activity – the men are taking a great gamble to prove their courage. What would be the point if everyone saw that a woman could do the same?'

Is this still about sport? In 1896 Cambridge male students celebrated the refusal to grant women degrees by hanging an effigy of a woman riding a bicycle, while in Mariah Burton Nelson's *The Stronger Women Get, the More Men Love Football* she wrote about how the growing popularity of lifting weights and bulking up among men coincided with an increased female presence in traditionally male domains.

In the last decade of the 1800s, the ideal male body as portrayed in advertisements put on about two dozen pounds. Men gave birth to the 'he-man.' The he-man was a redundant man, a man dedicated to the celebration of maleness. If women were determined to act like men, the ante would be upped: a woman could never be a he-man.

In a similar vein, females groupies may find themselves punished for making themselves available, for wanting 'it' as much as the players do. Jacquelin Magnay hinted at this, writing that 'many women aggressively pursue the players and record a notch on the wall when they score with one. But there is a code among some players that "bonus" points are given if women are shared among their mates; the more mates, the more points, and the more laughter afterwards.' In response to women upping the ante, becoming more like 'lads' in their pursuit of a score, it is as if certain groups of men have gone a step further in an attempt to reclaim their territory and diminish 'her' conquest in comparison to theirs.

In this sense, a woman defines a man. And if football *really is* just about men – as many insiders I spoke to claimed, seeing this as reason to leave it alone – then this book would be a waste of space. But it's not just about men. Women have been used – as have homosexuals, aka faggots and poofters – to reinforce a certain code of masculinity and hierarchy.

As court resumed and I watched Justin approach the dock, his shoulders hunched, I realised that boys have been used as well – used to win, to bolster kingpins and egos, and discarded when no longer of use. You could even say that in being denied

the genuine and equal company of women, they've been abandoned. Giving the guard a small, weak smile, Justin entered the
dock, sat down and took a deep breath.

# PART 4
# END GAME

# CHAPTER 21

Prosecutor Ryan called them the 'Mount Eliza Drinking Team' and it was as if the cast of *Home and Away* had found itself on the set of *Law and Order*. Suntanned boys in tight suits, their jauntiness lost somewhere between shirt cuffs and collar, girls in smart business-like dresses but still managing to look raccoon-eyed and rickety on their heels. This group of friends, who started off grand final day with a barbeque in Mount Eliza, then headed to a twenty-first and then Eve nightclub, before finding themselves back at Nate's house in Dorcas Street, was asked one by one to recount their evening.

It was a tale of boozy weaving, the group separating and meeting up again, a murky haze of shots, vodka and raspberry, and beer, the endless hailing of taxis, stops at McDonald's and walks to 7-Eleven – while for a couple of the boys, the evening turned into a comedy of errors as they were repeat-edly locked out of friends' places, unable to get a mate passed out inside a flat to open the door, returning into the night, only to be locked out of another house as they cabbed and walked all over town, trying to find somewhere to crash.

But each of them, at one or more times of the night, had seen a tall blonde girl in a colourful dress: Sarah.

Andrew Patterson had seen Sarah standing out the front of Dorcas Street, near the open door, chatting with John McCarthy. 'It was casual as saying goodbye,' he recalled. 'Pretty sure she was led out by John McCarthy. Just normal, like she was leaving a normal house.'

Then came Matthew Bateman, a solid bloke who held the Bible like a football when he was sworn in, his fingers spidering around it. After last drinks were called and the lights were turned on at Eve, he and his friend Megan went to Dorcas Street. No one answered when they buzzed on the intercom, but they knew where the spare key was hidden, so they let themselves in.

Some members of the Mount Eliza Drinking Team – a tag that was beginning to wear thin as the procession rolled on – were already there. They hung out upstairs and at one stage Bateman, Nate and a friend decided to walk down to 7-Eleven to grab some food, their route passing each of the potential laneways where Sarah and Justin could have been.

It was dark, Bateman said, but the sun was coming up. At one point he glanced down an alley and saw two people.

'Did you see anything that concerned you?' asked Malcolm Thomas.

'No, I would have stopped otherwise.'

The third on their mission to 7-Eleven, Toby Davis, a young, smartly dressed Asian man, also saw two people in an alley. Stopping to tie up his shoelaces, he glanced down the lane.

It was just over Cecil Street, he recalled – the laneway of Kathy Hackett – but it was just a 'glance.'

At the house, Davis recalled seeing the blonde girl in a 'bright floral dress' talking on the stairs to a guy in a 'scarf T-shirt.' Justin was wearing a T-shirt with a scarf screen-printed on it – 'an unfortunate choice,' Ryan said at one point, having a go at Justin's fashion sensibilities as he sat in the dock behind him.

On their way back from 7-Eleven, Davis said they saw the man in the scarf T-shirt and the girl in the floral dress getting into a taxi.

Jake Bergin was next to give evidence, then Celia Talbot. They had arrived together at Dorcas Street around 6 a.m. Bergin saw a blonde girl in a colourful dress walking down the hallway 'by herself' and noticed she was smiling. After passing her, he and Celia remarked to each other that she seemed 'happy for this time in the morning.'

*

'It's not going to her credit, that's for sure,' said Judge Taft at one stage while the jury was out, and it was not. The night was loaded with doubt, glazed with booze. The jury members were starting to look bored as they heard about twenty-first birthday parties, tequila shots and drunken walks punctuated by hollering at taxis to pick them up, all ending up at a house owned by the parents but lived in by their children – sounding more and more like a tale of privilege and dumb hopeless drunken journeys than a narrative of rape.

But as in any good soap opera, the outsiders were the conflict-makers. The tall blonde girl whom nobody knew and a country footballer.

Toby Davis's evidence was double-edged. It supported Justin's claims that he and Sarah had made contact inside the house and left together, contradicting the version put forward by the prosecution – that Justin, a stranger, had sidled up beside Sarah on the street – but he also placed the two people he had seen in the lane where Kathy Hackett lived.

Hackett was a small woman with a fringe and long brown hair. Her body was wiry, tough like a piece of beef jerky.

In the witness box, she sat up straight and looked around the court, at the judge and at Ryan.

'Were you asleep?' the prosecutor asked.

'Yeah!' Hackett responded enthusiastically. 'I was.'

'But you were woken?'

'Yeah – I was.'

Of the night traffic down her alley, Hackett said, 'I usually hear 'em laughing and walking down the laneway.' This time she heard a male and a female. 'It sounded like they were arguing underneath my window. I was rather peed off.' She went to the door and stood there for about three minutes before going back to bed. 'Then I heard "Don't," then "Leave me alone," then I heard clip-clops. Like a sandal, with a big heel, not a small heel.'

During Ryan's questioning, Malcolm Thomas did not look at Hackett. Instead he focused on a pile of documents in front of him, scribbling something on a piece of paper. But when Ryan sat down, it was as if Thomas drew himself up out of his chair, making himself a sudden presence in the room, his eyes practically swallowing the small witness in the box.

Thomas asked how Hackett had learned that the police wanted to speak to her.

'I had been down the street, my son said the police had been here, and I said, "What for?" He handed me the card, I called, and they came down immediately.'

Thomas raised his eyebrows. He asked Hackett how old her son was at the time.

'Twenty-two,' she replied

Thomas paused, glancing at the jury. Not a child, he may as well have said, not too young to be asked questions by the police before they asked to speak to anyone else in the house. As Thomas cross-examined, you could practically see him looping a length of rope around the feet of witnesses, who were oblivious until he tugged on it with a final question, the lasso tightening around their ankles and tripping them up.

Thomas asked, 'He didn't tell you how he'd spoken to the police?'

Hackett shook her head vehemently. 'He just handed me the card … he just said they said, "Get your mother to ring."'

And when she phoned the policeman, asked Thomas, did they tell her then what they were investigating?

'He goes, "Do you mind if I come around to your house and talk to you?"' replied Hackett.

Thomas shook his head. 'Look, that's not true, is it?'

Hackett would not budge. 'I didn't say anything over the phone. He came to my house and that's when we spoke and I told him – because when he first told me what had happened, I felt sick to the stomach about it.'

Thomas again shook his head. 'Can I suggest to you that it is simply not true that there was no discussion about what the police were investigating in that phone call?'

Thomas referred to a police note that said an officer had spoken to Hackett on the phone. He read from it: 'Female heard a female voice in laneway on Sunday morning, said "Don't," went to investigate but nil seen.'

Hackett shook her head vigorously. 'That was not on the phone. That was face to face. That was not on the phone.'

Thomas kept going. 'So how did you know what to tell the police if you didn't know what they wanted?' he asked. 'What may you have heard before that phone call to the police? Were you watching the news from time to time?'

'I don't have time to be watching anything,' she said. 'I go to work, I come home, I iron, I cook tea and it's time for me to go to bed. I'm lucky if I see any of the TV.'

Thomas nodded sympathetically. 'You weren't working then, were you?'

'No.'

'So you didn't have so little time in your day?'

Hackett's voice rose as if no one could understand her plight. 'I still don't have any time in my day. I'm a mother … I'm a mum and I do things every day of the week and I don't have time to be sitting there watching TV twiddling my thumbs … I have four children and two grandchildren.'

Thomas persisted. 'Too busy to watch TV, listen to the radio … and too busy to ever read the paper?'

Hackett snorted. 'I don't believe in the paper anyway because it's a whole lot of hogwash.' The court laughed.

'Too busy to chat to anyone about anything in the news?'

The rope, it was tightening, tightening, but Hackett was nimble. She replied, 'It's no one else's business, not mine.'

Thomas decided to ask her straight up. 'I'm just asking you about what you may have heard prior to that phone call from the police and let's put it this way: what you say is that you've heard absolutely nothing about any news?'

'The only thing I have heard,' said Hackett, 'which I thought was a whole lot of hogwash, is it's all the Collingwood players, it's all the Collingwood players because everyone always blames the poor Collingwood players.'

Bam. Got her.

Thomas drove it home. 'When you made your statement, it's in your mind that a sexual assault has occurred.'

'Not until after I said what I heard,' said Hackett. 'Halfway through my statement I knew.'

Thomas pointed out that in Hackett's original police statement she made no reference to clip-clop noises. 'You hear "footsteps,"' he said.

'I gather she was running off,' said Hackett.

'Of course you gather that,' said Thomas, looking at the jury, 'because you had been told a sexual assault had occurred in your laneway.'

Thomas sat down.

\*

Like Kathy Hackett's, Rajan Adani's dealings with star footballers or students living at college were likely to be brief at best.

In Adani's case, no more than a short taxi fare. Starting his shift just before 6 a.m., Adani stopped to pick up Justin and Sarah. It seemed an ordinary fare until the police tracked him down a week later. 'They were sitting very close,' Adani told the police. 'They were talking very gently and slowly.'

And he had been reliving it ever since – from giving his statement to the committal hearing, until now, over a year later, at the trial.

Softly spoken, the cabbie sat nervously in the witness box and described the journey. 'They were both deciding between Elwood and Carlton; he said his house was closer. In Elwood, he paid his fare and got out of the car. She got out too. I was wondering, you know, if I was going to lose a fare.'

Then, after a couple of minutes, she got back into the cab. Adani recalled the boy leaning in and giving her a goodbye kiss. He then drove her to Carlton.

'The boy leaned in and gave her a goodbye kiss,' repeated Thomas.

\*

Outside in the foyer, I was sitting next to Justin's older brother when John McCarthy came over. Tall and striking in a suit, the young footballer had been delisted by Collingwood last year and snapped up by Port Adelaide. The only one not called on to give evidence, he was also the only one from the night, let alone from Justin's Melbourne circle, to show up to support him.

'Listen to this,' he said to Justin's brother, and read from his phone a story about a violin player who sat in a subway station in Washington and played. Thousands of people had walked past him, paying no attention.

'No one knew this but the violinist was Joshua Bell, one of the best musicians in the world,' read McCarthy. 'He played one of the most intricate pieces ever written, with a violin worth 3.5 million dollars.'

McCarthy stopped reading and lowered his phone. 'And two days before, he had played a sold-out show where people were paying $100 a seat.'

Justin's brother was confused. 'What's your point?'

McCarthy was a little taken aback, not realising he'd have to explain it. He thought for a second. 'Well, if you don't pay attention, you might miss out on something amazing,' he said, then shrugged and walked away. Six months later, the 22-year-old midfielder was dead. John McCarthy fell from the roof of a Las Vegas hotel while on an end-of-season footy trip and could not be revived.

# CHAPTER 22

Can males bond without it becoming sinister? Of course they can. In the *Age*, Timothy Boyle, a former AFL player, described meeting his two best mates – Brad Sewell and their former teammate Luke Brennan – for a coffee. When the time came to say goodbye:

> Brad shook Luke's hand as if making his acquaintance anew (a handshake is off-limits while still in the playing group).
>
> 'Well, good to see you,' Brad said. 'Let's catch up soon.' They're ghastly social words that mean: 'I don't know when I'll see you next.'
>
> He didn't say anything to me until he'd closed his car door and was already driving. 'What time we on tomorrow?' He yelled it out the window, knowing that he needn't say goodbye – there wouldn't be enough time between seeing me to warrant it.

This is a mateship that doesn't need a hello, goodbye or a catch-up; it simply flows from one moment to the next as fluid as passing a ball. This familiarity and ease with one another is no doubt one of the deepest pleasures of such intense team bonding. Yet this same bond can be corrupted – it can see night games turn ugly. In a world where camaraderie is premised on a code of silence, it can become a bond that won't flex, and young men are not joined together by a love of the game but by secrets. And here, in this cloying space, it may become impossible to breathe.

Football has changed, yes. It is impossible to turn back the clock to the old days of full-time boilermakers and the like coming together each week to blow off steam. Players have gone from sipping Stone's Ginger Wine and nips of port during a game to beat the cold, sucking on ciggies in the huddle, to being surrounded by sport scientists, chaperones, player agents and dieticians who are constantly pinching and measuring the rolls of skin around their waist. If the old days were a bad time for individualism, then today it's near-apocalyptic. As the game is increasingly professionalised, players are programmed to within an inch of their lives, and when there are thousands of hopefuls who will give anything to take your place on the team, any desire to speak up or out of line may be rapidly quashed.

Football has always been thought of as the great leveller, a place where a kid from the backblocks has as much chance as a kid who has everything. For Tony Wilson, this adage still holds. 'The worst mistake in this whole debate is the assumption that there is this homogenous footballer. Footy introduced me to a much wider world, to men for whom footy was their ticket out,' he said. 'You could say it's bad to spend fifteen-odd years in the company of men, but I spent time with men who I'd never have met otherwise.'

Wilson tells me the story of when he was struggling to stay listed at Hawthorn, and Dermott 'The Kid' Brereton, then a senior and celebrated player, put his finger on what may have been holding the young player back. 'Tony, you got good hands, you can mark and you're brave,' said Brereton, 'but I wonder, what with you studying law, etc. … If I hadn't have been playing footy, I would be in jail. And I wonder if you would hurt like that to get where I am.' Brereton had a clear sense of where he would have been without footy, explained Wilson – while he, Tony, had choices. He wasn't hungry enough.

And indeed this is what makes football special. It is a chance, an opportunity for glory, in a life that sometimes may hold little other promise of that. But what happens when some of these kids go on to become known by their teammates, clubs and fans as the 'King' or 'God'? And when having sex with girls, especially the same girl, becomes a kind of off-field levelling among players? She's the ball and everyone gets a touch – that is, if they're 'hungry' enough. So have social distinctions really been done away with? It seems there are rankings in the darker stirrings of the football world, and it's got nothing to do with class. And it's in this murky territory where boys can become someone's fucked-up idea of men.

\*

One of the Mount Eliza Drinking Team was giving her evidence when the court suddenly started to fill up. Distracted, she faltered with her answers, looking past the lawyers to the heavy door that kept opening and shutting to reveal yet another reporter. Soon the questioning was over and the next witness was called.

Dayne Beams.

'How do you guys always know when to turn up?' I wanted to ask the journalist sitting next to me, but the star attraction was already making his way to the witness box. He was smirking, as if sucking in a smile. I figured he'd had to run a press gauntlet to get into the courthouse, and so his swagger was already warmed up. His renowned sleeve tattoo was hidden beneath a navy blue suit.

Plonking himself down on the chair, he swivelled it away from the judge and faced the wrong direction – looking at all of us in the court seats. Ryan stood up and cleared his throat. Swinging in the chair, Beams looked at the redheaded man with his pink cheeks, wearing a white wig and gown, and smiled a little.

The prosecutor began his questioning as he had with all the witnesses. Where were you prior to Eve, he asked, a simple question that harboured no trap, and yet Beams was defensive.

'I'm not sure,' he quipped.

Confused, Ryan asked again.

'I'm not sure,' Beams said.

Ryan decided to start at Eve instead. He asked how drunk Beams was when he left. 'I would have been drunk, but not extremely drunk,' said Beams.

Ryan turned to Dorcas Street. 'While you were in the house, did you see Justin Dyer?'

'Yes,' said Beams. 'He was with somebody … They were walking down the stairs, holding hands. She was blonde and she was tallish.'

Like all the witnesses from the Dorcas Street house, Beams had been warned not to reveal any of what had happened in the bedroom, yet he seemed to be going the extra mile, feigning ignorance and talking about this blonde female 'somebody.' But at the same time it was an act he seemed only partially to bother with – a half-smile kept pushing up the corner of his mouth, a kind of I-know-that-you-know-that-we're-all-full-of-shit smirk.

A few minutes later, Beams said he saw them again when he was jumping into a cab. 'I seen Justin Dyer and he was kissing the blonde female girl on the corner of the street.'

'Where were you?' asked Ryan.

'I was outside.'

But where, Ryan wanted to know.

'I'm not sure.'

Ryan looked at Judge Taft. He asked to make an application without the presence of the jury or witness. The judge nodded and Beams was told to wait outside, and the jury members were sent to their room at the back. The court was still full of reporters.

'In my respectful submission,' said Ryan, 'Mr Beams constitutes an unfavourable witness.'

Taft looked at Ryan sternly. 'Let me make it clear to you,' he said slowly, 'that I regard the slope you are facing as having a pretty steep incline.'

Ryan disagreed. He rummaged around in the papers on his desk until he found the right document. 'Your Honour has a copy of the conversation he had?' he asked. The judge nodded. Gesturing behind him at the full court, with a slight flick of his wig towards the suddenly interested press, Ryan said: 'For the purposes of this exercise I will do it in a silent method.'

Taft looked at the document in front of him. 'Yes, thank you.'

Ryan said, 'The assertion that he saw Justin Dyer "walking down the stairs" with a female "holding hands" does not appear in his version of events on that first occasion. Rather he says he saw him, his observation of him, was outside the dwelling, not inside the dwelling.'

Ryan was in a bind. He wanted to reveal to the jury that Beams's evidence had altered since he'd spoken to police and to suggest that he was covering up for his mate – but by law he could not cross-examine his own witness without dispensation from the judge.

The judge made a ruling on the spot against clarification. 'White-line fever should be avoided from every perspective,' he said. 'The application is refused.'

Beams and the jury were called back in.

Unable to cross-examine, Ryan's only other option was to get Beams out of the witness box as soon as possible. He wrapped up as soon as Beams sat down. For a moment, the baton was passed to Thomas, who glanced up from his papers and said, 'No questions, Your Honour.'

As Beams walked out of the courtroom, the tide of reporters stood and followed him. Ryan turned around, facing the open door, his face redder than usual, and said, 'Well, that was a fizzer,' before slumping down in his chair.

*

From interstate Scott Dempster, Justin's flatmate, appeared on the screen above the witness box. Dempster told the court that

Beams had invited him and Justin to Nate's house. Taxis were scarce, and when one did finally stop, it couldn't fit them all in. Dempster and one of the girls decided to walk.

It took fifteen, maybe twenty minutes to get to the house on Dorcas Street. When he got there, Dempster saw Justin outside with a girl. According to Dempster, Justin called out 'Scotty!' and then kissed the girl. The next day, he said, at their flat in Elwood, Justin told him he'd had sex with the girl.

When Thomas stood up, he had only one question to ask – Ryan had done all the hard work, much of it to the prosecution's detriment.

'Justin said to you that afternoon that the girl was planning on coming over later in the afternoon?'

Dempster nodded. 'Yes.'

\*

I was ready to hate him when Nate Cooper took the stand. Judge Taft sharply told him to sit down after he swore on the Bible. Cooper was tall with blue eyes. He gulped nervously as he peered around the courtroom.

He lived in Dorcas Street with his sister and his cousin, John McCarthy.

'Was part of your reasoning to go to Eve to meet up with Sarah?' asked Ryan.

'No, not at the time, no,' said Nate. 'I'd met her before, once.'

Again the narrative drew a blank as Ryan skipped over what happened in the bedroom.

'Now there came a time when Sarah left?' said Ryan.

'Yes.'

'Do you know when?'

'No.'

'Do you remember saying goodbye to her?'

'No.'

I wanted to slap him. Why hadn't he seen her out? Why didn't he say goodbye? He was the one who had brought her home to this mess. I was simmering with anger when Nate gave Judge Taft a pleading look. 'Excuse me, Your Honour,' he said in a breaking voice, 'can I please ask for a glass of water?' The anger in me eased off a little. The judge, too, seemed to soften. The court watched as Nate took the glass of water, his hand shaking, and gulped it down.

'At some point did you leave 303 Dorcas Street?' asked Ryan.

'Yes, with two mates,' said Nate. 'We went to 7-Eleven on Clarendon Street.'

'Did you notice anything on your way back?'

'I saw Justin and Sarah … I imagine I would have said "Hi."' The glass was empty, but Nate still held onto it tightly.

Just a boy, I thought. I remembered something I had heard a man say on the radio show *This American Life*. The interviewer had asked him why, when he was a teenager, he hadn't intervened when his friend had pulled a gun on another teenager. The man was quiet for a moment. Then, sighing, he said:

You gotta remember, Johnny, now we're big, now we're men – but we weren't men then, we thought we were men, but we were still kids.

Perhaps one of the most dangerous things is a kid who thinks he is a man. Will this line-up of boys reflect on this night in the same way? Nate sat wide-eyed in front of the judge, his mother and sister looking on, their hands in tight knots. Like Justin's family, did they think all of this was 'the girl's' fault, a slut who was now making their boy's life hell? Or were they looking at Nate anew? Uneasy, were they wondering how he had found himself in such a situation? Had he brought Sarah home with the intention of 'sharing her'? Or did the others enter his bedroom uninvited and he just move aside, letting them in?

At the end of his evidence, Nate, his mother and sister left the courtroom. There was no hanging around. And I wondered how much his mother knew and how much she refused to know. Did she feel as though she had failed, and that maybe, in the same way that her son had not respected Sarah, he did not respect her?

\*

'She's lying,' Justin's grandma hissed in my ear out in the foyer when the court took a break. 'She slept with four others that night, you know that? Four.'

I didn't know what to say anymore, so I said nothing.

\*

Dr Angela Williams was introduced to the court as a forensic expert, having done up to 1000 examinations. She had examined

Sarah Wesley at the Royal Women's Hospital on the Sunday of the allegations. Her evidence was brief. Ryan had few places to go with her as he was not allowed to venture into territory that could be easily explained away as evidence from the house, while for the defence the absence of Justin's semen could have been helpful only if he had denied having sex with Sarah. The lawyers tried to find their way through the minefield.

'What you do is look very specifically at a person's body? You write down what you see?' asked Thomas.

'Yes,' said Williams, 'and sometimes what we don't see.'

Thomas was only just getting started, but within moments the jury was dismissed. Judge Taft peered down at Thomas.

'Where are you going with this?' he enquired.

Thomas read from Sarah's police statement describing how she had said 'No' to the person in the alleyway, how it wasn't violent but she couldn't leave.

'Is it not consistent with what she says?' asked Taft, meaning Sarah's recent testimony.

'In relation to the alleyway?'

'Yes.'

'Arguably it's not,' said Thomas, 'if one is being grabbed and dragged.' If she was telling the truth, he was asking, then where was the physical evidence?

The jury was brought back in, and Thomas asked if there had been a pattern of fingermarks on Miss Wesley's arm. Dr Williams said no, there were no markings on the left or right arm. On the right elbow, she noted, there was a 1.5 cm bruise. It was red, which meant it could be either very young or days old. She added that everyone bruises differently and it was important to remember that an 'absence of an external sign doesn't indicate lack of trauma.'

Thomas nodded, thanked Dr Williams and sat down.

\*

'Are you with the victim?' a thin grey-haired woman asked Carol in the court foyer.

Justin's mum responded ferociously, 'It depends on who you think the victim is.'

The court volunteer quickly backtracked as it dawned on her that the family of the defendant was seated all around her. 'Oh yes, that is true.'

I silently tried to urge the woman away, to signal she was about to step on an ant's nest, but she kept talking. 'Oh yes, well, I'm a child of the sixties. Back then you'd never have seen the things that come up before the court today – but it is hard getting the balance right. Once we had a woman come in here at the same time as her alleged attacker and she just fainted away –'

'I would have laughed,' said Carol coldly.

'Mum,' said Justin.

'No, I mean it, I would have laughed in her face.'

'Mum,' Justin said again, but Carol kept going, her face cold and closed and unforgiving.

Justin rose and walked away down the corridor.

# CHAPTER 23

Justin was wearing a maroon rugby jumper and was slumped at a grey table. His hands rested in front of him as the policewoman informed him of his rights. He looked stunned. This wasn't what he'd expected. It wasn't supposed to be him the police were interested in. He thought he was here to talk about what had happened inside the house. At least that was the impression he had received from Beams, whom he'd spoken to earlier in the day, the AFL footballer telling Justin to see David Galbally, Collingwood's lawyer, before going to the station. Galbally hadn't mentioned this turn of events either. Justin had arrived with a statement he'd typed out with the Collingwood lawyer and expected to be able to leave it at that. Instead, he was ushered into an interview room. He had the right to say nothing and to request a lawyer, but he shook his head. He was happy to talk. The footage flickered a little.

Instead of Justin giving his evidence in the witness box, the defence decided to play the video of his original police statement. My story hasn't changed, Justin said to me outside court when I asked why. 'Malcolm thinks this way is better.' This way, I later discovered, the prosecution could not cross-examine him. Justin looked younger in the video, the edges around his face softer. It was Monday night and the news was still awash with highlights and analysis of the grand final. It had been some thirty-six hours since Justin got out of the cab and said goodbye to Sarah.

'Now, as we talked about,' said the officer, 'it is an allegation of rape.' She asked Justin to explain what had happened.

'We rocked up,' said Justin, outlining how he arrived at the house, that he needed to go to the loo and had asked where the toilet was. Then the tape skipped a little. Justin was now describing talking to Sarah. 'Struck up a conversation, she said she was going to walk home, from South Melbourne to Carlton, "Not going to let you walk to Carlton."'

Justin explained that walking down Dorcas Street he still hadn't been to the loo and ducked into a laneway to take a piss.

'Called her into the lane,' he said, 'we had sex. Then she stopped and said, "I've gotta go to this party." She took about two steps and I caught her hand, "Can you finish me off?" She said okay, and then stopped, said she had to go to a barbeque or something.'

Justin called her about an hour later to see if she had got home alright. 'This guy picked up and said she's sleeping. She'd promised she'd come over around 4 p.m. Called back, texted, I didn't hear back from her. I haven't heard from her.'

The tape cut out then reopened, like an eye.

The police officer asked him to go over the events again in more detail.

Justin said that 'Coops' opened the door for him at the Dorcas Street house. 'I only know him as "Coops."'

This, it turned out, was Nate's nickname. Justin started talking to Sarah at the top of the stairs. 'How you going? What's your name? Where you from?'

That kind of thing, he said. As Justin talked, I noticed that his voice neither rose nor fell, but remained at the same constant quiet level – it was his hands that moved, as if marking the emphases. He splayed them, palms up, as if surrendering.

Justin said he was at Dorcas Street for about fifteen, twenty minutes. When they left, he saw Scott Dempster out the front and called to him, then started kissing Sarah.

'She was already halfway up the alley when I was pissing,' he said. 'I had a few drinks, couldn't really get my penis hard, had a couple go's, fell out.'

The officer wanted to know if he was drunk.

'Drunk? I felt alright. I knew what was going on.'

The officer then pressed for more detail. 'Rubbing her vagina, she was rubbing me, come down here, I undid my pants and she dropped to her knees, I asked if we could have sex, she bent over – maybe ten, fifteen seconds, then she went down again, did it more and then she said, "I really gotta go."

'"Can you finish me off?" She said yes. I thought if she didn't want to do it, she would've said no.

'She turned around, lifted her dress up and pulled her undies down,' Justin continued. 'I didn't do it. I didn't intimidate her. I don't intimidate girls.'

Justin's hands were face up on the table. They flared up with his last sentence, his fingers curling, and then lay back flat. The video flickered again and cut out for keeps this time. All those little erased bits, I thought, hovering around like question marks.

\*

Two detectives arranged to meet Justin at the alleyway after his police statement. They parked on Dorcas Street, just near the townhouse, wearing a wiretap. The 'covert' recording was played in court. One of them phoned Justin to ask where he was – you could hear his faint, tinny reply. At the laneway, he said. He had parked his Holden ute outside the Commonwealth Bank on Clarendon Street. The officers walked down the street, past the two laneways they'd been looking at, to meet him. For about five minutes the court listened to the clip-clopping of the female detective's heels.

When they saw him, he was standing at the mouth of Emerald Hill Place, just off Clarendon Street. 'You're not under arrest,' the detectives reminded him, protecting themselves and the recording. 'You don't have to be here. You don't have to say anything. We invited you here.'

You could practically hear him nod. 'It's just here,' he said and he sounded polite and fragile now that we knew he was being recorded without his knowledge.

\*

On the stand, Senior Detective Constable Christine Stafford said that when Justin Dyer identified Emerald Hill Place as the alleyway and even indicated where he'd urinated, the sexual crimes squad had taken swabs of the area, only to discover later that DNA would not show up in less than a litre of urine.

She described taking Sarah for a D/O, a drive-over, after meeting her at the Royal Women's Hospital. Together they drove around South Melbourne looking for a 'newish townhouse.'

When they found it, they began looking for the alleyway. Sarah remembered 'cobblestones and high walls' – Justin's alley had both, and Kathy Hackett's had cobblestones with a high wall on one side and a fence on the opposite.

And as the questioning began to drag on, police officers reading from their notebooks and young twenty-somethings reciting how much they had to drink, you could tell the novelty had worn off for the jury. It had been ten days of shuffling in and out of the courtroom – of strange applications, legal matters that needed to be discussed without them, blind spots that no one asked about. So when Judge Taft called stumps, you could see that they were relieved.

Thomas tabled the phone records for Sarah, Justin and Tom Shaw, and then it was time for the closing addresses.

# CHAPTER 24

Prosecutor Ryan began. And again the courtroom felt alive with nerves: finally we were getting to the guts of the matter.

'The onus is on the Crown to prove,' he said, 'while the accused man need prove nothing.'

He started with the laneways. Was the relevant laneway the one closest to Cecil Street, where Kathy Hackett lived, as supported by both Toby Davis's and Matthew Bateman's testimonies? The same laneway, he added, suggested by Sarah's statement at the hospital – Detective Stafford had noted 'cobblestones that she ran across to run away from the accused.' 'You have to remember,' Ryan reminded the jury, 'that she had been awake for twenty hours.'

Thomas and his defence team all had their heads down, busy scribbling notes.

Ryan told the jury that it had been put to Kathy Hackett, resident of the alley, that her mind had been poisoned in some way. But Hackett had *volunteered* her information to the police.

'The accused man got it wrong when he identified the laneway. He had had twenty-odd drinks. His account is just as affected as the Mount Eliza Drinking Team's,' said Ryan, pausing. He then raised his eyebrows at the jury. 'And yet, when you read his account, it is flawless, a chronological account. When you analyse his account of events, it is contrary to human experience.

'This incident happened in the laneway next to Kathy Hackett's house,' said Ryan, hammering the air with his hand, bleary-eyed but determined.

Now, Justin's arrival at Dorcas Street, said Ryan. He walked up the stairs, asking where's the toilet, even undoing his fly. 'It's a matter of urgency,' said Ryan, 'he's busting. But then he talks to everyone else instead.'

'He was so struck by his physical attraction to her that he forgot to go to the toilet,' said the prosecutor, disbelievingly. 'And she says, "I'm walking home" – now, let's look at the shoes she was wearing.' Ryan referred to the photo of Sarah's high heels. 'One thing you can bet on is that she did not say she was walking home.'

I stifled a laugh at this. Only a man would say this and only a jury full of men would consider believing it. Every woman knows that females walk miles in heels, especially when drunk.

Ryan continued: 'This is about commonsense, experience of life. He's been in the house for five minutes, busting to go to the loo but doesn't go, and then in the next instance, he's having a sexual act with her.

'A "blonde bombshell" in a matter of moments,' said Ryan, shaking his head. 'It doesn't ring true.'

The jury was riveted. 'I will walk you, fair damsel, to get a cab to Carlton, then in a matter of fifty metres it's my hand down her dress,' Ryan scoffed.

'How romantic, ladies and gentlemen,' he announced, spinning around to face the court, 'in a pool of urine Sarah Wesley drops to her knees to suck a stranger's penis. What nonsense.'

She 'turned around, pulled her dress up, pulled her pants down.' Again Ryan scoffed: 'She certainly is a sport.'

Justin's family turned to look at him searchingly, trying to read him – but Justin's face was blank. The jury was excused for a break, and Thomas stood up to make an objection. He reeled off some of Ryan's speech: 'Fair damsel, she's a sport, a fifty-metre relationship.' It was an extremely unfair approach, he said – particularly as she had had sex with x number of men beforehand, something the defence was not allowed to allude to. Taft listened to Thomas's objection, but was dismissive.

As the two talked, a lone female police officer who had given evidence earlier entered the court and sat in a seat behind the prosecution. The seats around her were empty. Still, no one had turned up for Sarah.

'They'll be here if he's convicted,' I was told on a later break by the police officer. 'To hear his sentencing.'

\*

'Now I'm going to tell you a story,' said Ryan to the jury, rocking back on his heels, 'and it's only in an Australian context. How do you know when someone is really a friend?'

He waited for a moment, letting the room fill with silence. Then he opened his mouth, puncturing the hush.

'When you say to them, "I just killed someone," and the friend responds, "Where should we bury the body?"'

I glanced over at Justin. He was staring at Ryan, mouth open.

'Dayne Beams and Scott Dempster are burying the body,' Ryan continued, 'the body of Sarah Wesley.'

Dempster, said Ryan, is lying. And as for Beams: 'He couldn't remember the convention centre where he went with his team to celebrate. Think of the things he says he sees. He gets into the cab and sees Justin kissing a girl.'

He's known Justin for a few years, said Ryan, before repeating ominously, 'Where do we bury the body?'

Carol stood up unsteadily. She looked as if she had been punched. She walked out of the courtroom. The jurors' eyes followed her out. Ryan paid no attention.

'Now, I want to take you to the complainant. She's a foreigner to people in the house. It doesn't seem that she is surrounded by a galaxy of friends.'

None, actually, I thought.

Ryan said that Sarah had not reacted in the way she thought she would have in such a situation: she had thought she'd fight back, but she didn't. 'She thought she'd be safer if she went along. We all have artificial expectations of ourselves,' Ryan said, his tone suddenly good-natured, 'I'm an old man in the mirror, but in my head I'm seventeen, twenty-two.'

Earlier, Ryan had mentioned the 1950s film *Kim*, starring Errol Flynn, to make a point, and now he started talking about a book called *The Singapore Grip*, a 1978 classic, he explained. The jury stared at him blankly as he outlined the book's plot, concerning the Japanese invasion and fall of Singapore in World War II. Ryan talked about the ups and downs, the pressure the island was under, how it was forced to surrender after the British rulers *capitulated*, abandoning Singapore to the enemy.

'Sarah Wesley capitulated,' says Ryan. 'She went with Justin Dyer – what was she to do?' In the taxi, he continued, she wanted to get into the front, but he said get in the back. He knew she capitulated.'

'Her memories are not intact,' Ryan conceded, while the accused's were 'ordered, chronological and in my view artificial.' He described how she got away and Justin caught up with her on the street, asking for her number. 'Having suffered what she suffered, she capitulated.'

Ryan looked at each juror, pushing the capitulation, the burying of the body. 'You will convict Justin Dyer,' he said finally, and sat down.

Justin looked pale. His girlfriend twisted in her seat to look at him, tried to catch his eye, but he just stared at Ryan in a daze.

# CHAPTER 25

Malcolm Thomas stood up. He handed the phone records to the jurors and then scratched his head.

'Now, I've been trying to work out if I was in primary school when Mr Ryan was doing this job,' he said, 'and trying to work out why such an experienced prosecutor would not say anything about these phone records, and then I realised why. It's best not to talk about them.'

'Well, I'm going to talk about them. That document,' Thomas said, pointing to the phone records, 'is an agreement between the complainant and the accused.'

Thomas went through the records, pointing out that there were no calls made from Sarah's phone.

'Not only,' said Thomas, 'but Tom Shaw is calling her. At 5.48 a.m., 5.53 a.m., 6.07 a.m., 6.36 a.m. and left a 48-second message.'

Now, said Thomas to the jury, forget all the witnesses, the conspiracy, the Beams and Dempster whatever. Sarah Wesley is a liar. 'What is she lying about? Where do her lies stop?' he asked. 'Lie after lie, and then other lies to explain those lies.'

In opening the case to the jury, Ryan had said Sarah tried to call Tom Shaw on her phone, but the records of her phone calls showed otherwise, Thomas stated. She didn't call him. Not only that, but she didn't need to call him – she could have just answered his calls.

Thomas read from the transcript of his cross-examination of Sarah regarding her phone records. 'Lie, lie, lie,' he said.

Thomas looked at the jury. 'Lie. And then we get to the last refuge of a lie. What is the last refuge of a lie? It's "I don't know, I can't remember." There is a difference between TV and real life,' said Thomas. 'On TV, she gets the phone records put to her and she breaks down, admitting that she's lied. But in real life, the lies dig in.

'And she lies to Tom Shaw too. She didn't say, "I was ignoring your calls, having a good time and couldn't be bothered getting back to you" – instead she lies.

'Control, says the prosecution. Everything that happened after the alley is about Justin maintaining control over her. He gave her his number, showed her where he lived. How does that maintain control? Now, Sarah got a message from Shaw saying they could come and pick her up. She got it as she was coming out of the alleyway – but instead she spends fifteen minutes on Clarendon Street trying to find a taxi with the man who supposedly just raped her.

'Why? Simple explanation. There's no need. He hasn't raped her. No need for concern. If you tell one lie, you have to tell another lie.

'So, we have this bloke who is supposedly in control – and he's just letting her ring?

'Now, why wouldn't you believe Mr Adani? He's not drunk, he's not part of the conspiracy. How lucky are we to have Mr Adani – if we didn't have him, you'd just have Mr Dyer's word against Miss Wesley's. Mr Adani is not connected to anyone, has no reason to lie.

'Mr Adani says they were talking "very gently and slowly," while Sarah denied she got out of the cab at Justin's place.' Thomas referred to Sarah's evidence in the committal hearing, her claim that she had pushed Justin away in the cab and said 'No' loudly. But in this trial she had failed to mention that, he said. 'Remember what I said about lies and digging their heels in?'

Thomas now turned to the alley. 'This isn't a capitulation,' he said, dismissing the prosecution's explanation for Sarah's behaviour. He reminded the jurors of her evidence: 'this is a violent struggle.'

Thomas mentioned Sarah's high heels and that she had never called out to anyone walking past. And yet, with his pants down – and here Thomas threw up his hands – Justin was supposed to have got in front of her three times. 'I don't mean to make light of it,' he said, 'but it's ridiculous.'

As for which alley, Thomas said, 'We'll never know for sure.' But Kathy Hackett was 'not the silver bullet. If you're not satisfied it's her laneway, then her evidence is worthless. Don't let evidence that doesn't fit be twisted around, bits pulled off it to make it fit.' And: 'You might think it very dangerous to put much weight on what she says. She remembers more, the more she is told.'

Now, said Thomas, as if dusting his hands of Kathy Hackett, the prosecution has to prove that 1) Sarah Wesley was not consenting at the time, and 2) Justin Dyer did not believe she was consenting.

'First, Justin spells his name out to her – "Here's my number." A course you take if you have consensual sex and you want to maintain contact. He gets in a taxi with her with independent witnesses, pays with his credit card and "Here's where I live." That behaviour is utterly consistent with a man who believed he just had consensual sex.

'Justin's account is plausible and consistent. In fact he is criticised because it is too consistent – but his account is consistent with the taxi driver's and phone records. Why is it all so plausible? Because it's the truth.'

Thomas pointed out to the jury that no evidence had been presented about the character of Sarah Wesley, and yet it had been suggested by the prosecution that she would not have done these things on such a brief acquaintance. But there was no evidence to prove this. Then, speaking the language of a younger generation, he added: 'People at a party hook up without any great conversation or otherwise.'

As Thomas began to wrap up, I looked at the jurors. Most of the men were middle-aged or older. I wondered what their idea of 'commonsense' was. It had been two and a half days of closing addresses. They looked admirably attentive given the long hours.

Thomas continued: 'Consent does not equal romance. It doesn't stop it being consensual because it was later regretted. There is a presumption of innocence in this country, it's real, it's important.'

Miss Wesley has lied, the defence lawyer repeated. If you

deliver any verdict other than not guilty, then later on you might think you're not so sure.

*

'There's an inherent improbability in the account offered by Mr Dyer,' Judge Taft had said. And it was true, it was doubtful Sarah turned around, pulled down her undies and bent over for Justin all by herself. Nor was it likely that she had got on her knees entirely of her own accord. Justin's hands would have been on her, guiding her. He wasn't a lamppost, inanimate, after all.

Justin's account seemed to me devoid of his own agency. But there were parts of his story that sounded plausible. Sarah stopping in the alley, saying she had to go to a party, his asking to be 'finished off.' It was dialogue you couldn't make up. As I looked over my notes at my observations of Justin, I realised I had little more than a pencil sketch of him. He was strangely passive. Had I failed to colour him in, or was he a cipher, a cardboard cut-out, a straggler separated from his herd? I thought about how, each time I tried to get his measure, it was like trying to calculate the depth of a peculiar body of water. He was neither shallow nor impossibly deep. All this time I had thought that Sarah was the ghost, the absent one in the story – but it was Justin. Lost in the blur of his team colours, he was the opposite of a criminal. He was extremely obedient. It was just that the rules of his world didn't match up with those followed by the rest of us.

# CHAPTER 26

Maybe I've got it all wrong. Maybe there is no common truth. The trial is black and white, Sarah and Justin are as one-dimensional as their competing storylines make out. You've got the rapist or the liar. A *Law and Order* version, and by trying to seek out a shade of grey I'm protecting one of them. That is not going to sit well with feminists or footballers, I think, a knot of dread in the pit of my stomach. I prepare myself for the accusations – that I'm a traitor to women for even suggesting that Sarah is not telling the exact truth, for not pointing the bone at Justin. I wish I'd chosen to follow an 'easier' rape trial – one with an obvious villain, where a female was clearly intoxicated beyond consent, where I could make observations that don't stink of the bad old days. But while every good story needs a villain, I can't make it Justin. He's been carved out of a pack. Whatever he did that night, he thought it was okay. The herd had said as much. Teams, after all, require a certain amount of groupthink to succeed.

And again, I wonder how much of myself I'm projecting onto Sarah. I may be filling her with my own failings, the teen-age me who failed to articulate myself, who absolved myself of the responsibility to say no *and* yes, who was complicit – I can see this now – in being treated badly. Something Ian Roberts said on ABC TV's *Australian Story* has stayed with me. Talking about his experience as a gay man in rugby league, he said:

> This is a tough thing to say but, you know, predominantly gay people want to be treated as equal but fail to treat themselves as equal.

If Sarah did not tell the truth, if she lied about explicitly telling Justin 'No' and that he pushed and dragged her, then I can only say that she chose a lie over what she perceived as her only other option, silence. She had no language to explain the grey zone, to explain what was lost in translation between the sexes.

It is as if there's a fear that venturing into a grey area to discuss the complexities of consent and rape will unravel some forty years of feminist spadework, that people will be unnecessarily confused by any such discussion. But surely feminism isn't that fragile. And isn't it obvious that people are already confused? For despite the law being clear on the definition of consent, neither the police nor the public prosecutors seem to have much faith in a jury's ability to convict in certain cases, even if they do satisfy the legal criteria.

The public idea of a rapist is, it seems, that of a twisted loner, most likely a male with an underlying mental illness, who seeks out his victims with the full intention of raping them. Popular footballers most certainly do not fit this category – and in spite of it making them extremely slippery to prosecute, that is a good thing. After all, the lone rapist shows little sign of changing. He has no culture, no friends and no support – and all of this makes him easier to convict, but it also makes him unanswerable. Society gave up on him, and he on society, a long time ago.

Players, however, who tread the grey zone of rape and treating women badly, can be made accountable. More than managed, they can be changed, if their codes make it so, if their clubs quit covering up and if the world of football stops being a sanctuary for tired old sentiments such as 'boys will be boys' and instead becomes a sanctuary for boys who not only want to play good football but also become good men in the process.

But now? For everything that Justin and his mates had been through, I couldn't say I detected a nuanced understanding of what had happened in the wee hours of the morning after the grand final, let alone any humility. Justin told me that he and his friends – including Dayne Beams – had changed since his rape charges. 'No more one-night stands,' he said. 'Not unless it involves a contract.' But was this indicative of true change? Sure, they might be more wary, but was it because they had reconsidered or simply had their beliefs about certain types of females affirmed? To them, Sarah is a liar, a bitch and a slut. And the disrespect and inhumanity with which they treated her and thought of her is one quality they may find themselves sharing with the lone rapist. Malice, after all, can be built on ignorance.

Court, it seems, is not where progress is made. It's just where things end up.

\*

The jury was almost ready to deliberate on Justin's fate. They were gathered before the judge one last time to receive his instructions before disappearing into the back room. Judge Taft outlined the charges. The central issue, he said, was whether Sarah did not consent and whether Justin was aware of her not consenting.

Each charge must be established beyond reasonable doubt – and the elements of each charge that must be proved are that Dyer sexually penetrated Wesley in the alleged way, that he did this intentionally, that Wesley did not consent, and that Dyer was aware that she was not consenting.

If you believe there is a possibility that Dyer believed Wesley was consenting, then the prosecution has failed in proving that element.

Consent, he said, means free agreement. Sarah Wesley says she did not consent and clearly conveyed that.

Taft reiterated the importance of 'beyond reasonable doubt.' 'Even if you think Mr Dyer is not telling the truth in his police interview,' he said, 'you put that aside and ask, is Sarah's evidence honest, accurate, reliable?'

The jury members left to begin their deliberations. It was 11 a.m. on a Tuesday. It was twelve days from when they had been selected. Twelve days since they had first encountered Sarah and Justin. Now they had to decide what to do with them.

*

It's a long wait.

The kind of wait where you imagine every possible scenario,

where each outcome is weighed, held to the light and checked underneath for markings, a sign of some sort.

I sit outside, with Justin and his family mostly, all day.

It's the kind of wait that clocks can't measure and yet when it hits 4.30 p.m., and the lights inside the locked courtroom go off, we stand and go home.

It's exhausting, this waiting.

In the morning, everyone is already there when I arrive. No one has heard anything.

The Dyer family sits, empty seats staggered between them, each alone with their thoughts. Justin's father, I learn, who has been on chemotherapy during the trial, has been taken to hospital in Queensland with chest pains.

Carol holds her phone close. He has been put on oxygen, she tells me.

The hours continue to pass, each one feeling like a drip slowly developing on a tap before pulling away and falling to the ground. Vanessa sits on her hands, rocking slightly. She says that last night she lay with Justin and wondered if it was for the final time.

Lunch comes and goes. Malcolm Thomas's confidence, his smooth swimming-pool surface, seems to crack a little – tiny waves of worry lapping. He begins to talk to Justin about jails, that the jail closest to his family on the Gold Coast is known for its violence and instability, that it's not an option he should consider applying for. He is told to expect about three years if they convict him.

Justin is pale and quiet. He goes to the toilet.

Then, abruptly, the journalists appear. The verdict is in.

And when the tipstaff unlocks the courtroom door, it's as if she is unlocking time. Justin stands up, but doesn't move. I wonder if he has to tell his legs to move, as if he is on a precipice and suddenly he wants to stay out here, in the dead space of this long wait. I hold my breath, watching him.

Finally, he moves. He enters the court and walks toward the dock.

# EPILOGUE

'I'm already sick of it,' said my neighbour when I said footy season was about to start, aware he was an avid AFL fan. We had stopped to commune over our green bins and his face soured at the mention of the game. Even in the off-season, he growled, football didn't stop. It was at the height of the St Kilda Schoolgirl affair, the media seemingly unable to focus on anything else, but his discontent was not solely the handiwork of an angry teenager. It was the belief that footy is more than just a game that annoyed him.

In 2010, the then Carlton captain, Chris Judd, won the Brownlow Medal. Known as an all-round good guy, he looked uncomfortable as he accepted AFL's highest honour at the televised black-tie and ball-gown affair. Standing on a podium, he answered questions from the event's host with the usual 'not really saying anything' air of a role-model footballer – but then he did something different.

'I think footballers and Brownlow medallists get put up on pedestals,' he said in response to the host's question of what it meant to win a Brownlow. 'Football, if you like, is sort of make-believe, it's like a self-indulgent pastime where you go out each week and announce to the football public the type of person you and your mates are. It's not real.'

Struggling to articulate himself, Judd clung to the oft-used example of the late Jim Stynes, a former player, then a club president, a philanthropist and youth worker, as doing valid work in the real world. When Judd paused, the room erupted into applause. But it felt like a smother. The host quickly moved on: 'You touched on it earlier, how tough was it to leave the West Coast Eagles?'

*

I need to swim laps every week. I need to run. Playing basketball is one of my greatest pleasures. This book is not anti-sport. 'Jock culture is a distortion of sports,' the American author and sports journalist Robert Lipsyte once noted, warning that America was in danger of finding its values in the locker room. It's not the game, the pleasure of play, that's dangerous. It's the piss stains in the grass, the markings of men who use sport as power and the people – teammates, fans, coaches, clubs, doctors, police, journalists, groupies – who let them do whatever they want.

Of course, this is not to say that all footballers are the same. But you don't have to look too far afield to see that there is a problem here – one that has the potential to become far more ugly if left unchecked.

In 2004, Lipsyte suggested at an American Psychiatric Association general meeting that 'psychiatry has not taken enough interest in jock culture as a window into other American pathologies.'

By dismissing sport 'as all fun and games,' he said, analysts were ignoring 'the values of the arena and the locker room [which] have been imposed on our national life.'

\*

Later, after the trial, I arranged to meet Justin at a shopping centre in the eastern suburbs. He had flown down from the Gold Coast to see his girlfriend. I waited outside one wintry morning for him to show up. He arrived with Vanessa, wearing thongs, jeans, a jumper and a beanie. 'He didn't bring any proper shoes with him,' his girlfriend said, laughing, pointing at his blue toes. 'He's already forgotten what it's like down here.'

At a café, we sat outside behind a clear plastic tarp and under the heaters. I asked him how he felt and he smiled: 'Better, so much better.' He confided that he had been suicidal after the charges were laid, that he had thought about driving his car fast and smashing it into a tree. 'Now, I wake up in the morning and remember that it's over. It's such a relief.'

When I asked if he and his footy friends talked trash about women when they hung out, he shook his head. 'No.'

Vanessa laughed and picked up Justin's hand. 'Yes, you do,' she said.

'What do you mean?' Justin asked her, looking surprised.

'I've heard you guys when you're all together. You say horrible things about chicks.'

Justin looked at her wide-eyed, then back at me. He shrugged. 'Maybe we do, but I guess 'cause I'm in it, I don't hear it like that.'

'So, what happened that night?' I wanted to know. 'In the bedroom. What happened?'

Justin sighed. 'It was stupid, really.' Vanessa leaned forward to listen.

'I walked up the stairs and got to the bedroom where there was stuff going on.' Someone opened the door and Justin walked in.

'And then the door shut behind me. It was dark and it was just Beams and the girl on the bed. I was like, what? Then Beams yelled at me to "Get out" and the door opened and McCarthy ran in. He turned the lights on, was saying, "Where's my tie?" They wanted to go to Tram nightclub and you need to wear a tie to get in. She was just in the bed and didn't seem to mind everyone, her boobs were showing, she didn't pull up the cover or anything.'

'Three of the guys had been with her,' said Justin. 'She got dressed and I struck up a conversation with her on the stairs, asked her how she was getting home. She said she was walking home, it was a strange thing' – Justin looked at me, shaking his head – 'but I thought, imagine if something happens to her.'

# ACKNOWLEDGMENTS

*Night Games* was far from a solo effort. I could not have written this book without the brave in-depth reporting of frontline journalists such as Sarah Ferguson, Ticky Fullerton, Jacquelin Magnay and Jessica Halloran. The same goes for the documentary-makers Rebecca Barry and Michaela Perske of *Footy Chicks* and Miriam Cannell of *Game Girls*.

A huge thank you to the Literature Board at the Australia Council for the Arts, whose generous Book2 Grant meant I was able to write *Night Games* without having to waitress a few nights a week. The only problem is that I've gotten used to this rather nice way of living – how do I go back to my old life?! Thanks also to *Griffith REVIEW* for giving me the Emerging Writers Prize, which included a week's residency at the wonderful Varuna.

The number of hands on deck for *Night Games* was outstanding.

No word went unturned, thanks to my team of readers: Sarala Fitzgerald, Julie Clayton, Sophy Williams, Bridget Costelloe, Erik Jensen, Peter Krien, Nick Feik, Sacha Krien and Tom McGuigan.

At my beloved stable, Black Inc., thanks to editor Nikki Lusk for her eagle eye and designer Peter Long for the striking cover. Also to my good friend and publicist Elisabeth Young – I'm so lucky to have you in my corner.

And of course, Chris Feik, my editor and right-hand man. You make me sound a hell of a lot smarter than I am.

Thanks also to Black Inc.'s lawyer, Geoff Gibson, whose sound advice and steady hand saw us skirt all manner of terrible scenarios.

Which brings me to the book's darkest hour, a difficult time in which I can't thank Helen Garner, Scott Spark and my honorary husband Benjamin Law enough for their support and solidarity.

And there's more.

In the middle of writing this book, I had a baby. Warmest thanks to my family and friends for helping juggle the little fella while I typed madly, in particular the beautiful Lesly Carbonell and my mother, Elisabeth Krien. Thanks also to my darling friend Romy Ash for organising a dinner roster in the first couple of weeks.

Thanks to my main man, Emilio, who held me up when all I wanted to do was fold and had to put up with me reading gloomy titles such as *The History of Rape* in bed at night. That was fun, wasn't it, honey?

And finally, my thanks to the people whose voices are in this book – be it on the page or behind the scenes. There are too many of you to thank individually, but you know who you are. People who spoke to me on and off the record, who trusted me, who told me things I didn't know and who helped clarify my thoughts – people who shared their wisdom, insights and contacts. Thank you.

# ABOUT THE AUTHOR

Anna Krien is the author of *Night Games: Sex, Power and a Journey into the Dark Heart of Sport*, which was shortlisted for the Stella Prize, the Adelaide Festival Award for non-fiction and the Walkley non-fiction award.